PURSUING
WISDOM

A BIBLICAL APPROACH FROM PROVERBS

KENNETH
BOA &
GAIL
BURNETT

NAVPRESS●
BRINGING TRUTH TO LIFE
P.O. Box 35001, Colorado Springs, Colorado 80935

The Navigators is an international Christian organization. Our mission is to reach, disciple, and equip people to know Christ and to make Him known through successive generations. We envision multitudes of diverse people in the United States and every other nation who have a passionate love for Christ, live a lifestyle of sharing Christ's love, and multiply spiritual laborers among those without Christ.

NavPress is the publishing ministry of The Navigators. NavPress publications help believers learn biblical truth and apply what they learn to their lives and ministries. Our mission is to stimulate spiritual formation among our readers.

TABLE OF CONTENTS

ACKNOWLEDGMENTS

Many thanks from Ken to Professor Bruce Waltke, whose teaching provided the original inspiration for many of the concepts presented in this book.

Many thanks from Gail to John Luther Baxter, my late grandfather, whose deep love for the Word was contagious. And many thanks to Kay Arthur of Precept Ministries, who taught me how to study. Finally, a special "I love you" to friends and family members who supported me during this year of writing—especially Shirley and Roy, Bonita and Grady, Donna and Ed, Steve, my children, and my parents.

TO THE SPIRITUAL TRAVELER

Suppose when you were small, your father had held a book in his hands and said, "When you are old enough, I'm going to give you this book. This is a book about truth, written by the wisest among men. For centuries it has withstood the scrutiny of great scholars, but none has ever proven it wrong. This book holds the secrets to all of life's challenges!

"Now remember, my child, although truth is ancient, it is also timeless. Therefore, these words are just as relevant today as when they were first spoken some three thousand years ago. How eager I am to give this book to you! It will guide you rightly and teach you to be wise. It will touch every facet of your life as it speaks of humility and pride, justice and vengeance, work and laziness, wealth and poverty, friends and neighbors, love and lust, anger and strife, masters and servants—even life and death. Yes, some day, when you are old enough. . . ."

You know, I'll bet you couldn't wait to get your hands on that book! How could any child resist such allure? It sounds like a page right out of some mystical fantasy, doesn't it? Yet every description rightly relates to the book of Proverbs. Proverbs is the wisdom of God revealed to us through the prophets and sages (the wise men and women of the Old Testament) and through the life of Christ.

Why, then, do most of us grow up more eager to learn to drive a car than to navigate our lives? Perhaps it's because the value of living our lives by the wisdom of God was not pressed upon us in our youth. But good news—it's not too late! We can begin right now to understand the deep truths of God. Follow God's command from Proverbs 4:5, "Acquire wisdom! Acquire understanding! Do not forget, nor turn away from the words of my mouth."

If you will apply yourself to a disciplined study of the Word of God, you can trust God to reveal Himself and His ways and to give you His eternal perspective, so you can see beyond your own limitations. My desire in ministry is to help you learn to observe the events of life and from them gain understanding and discernment. I want to lead you to the Source of truth, so you'll be able to act instead of react and to act *intelligently*—to think things through in relation to God's commands and to His revelation of Himself. Although there is tremendous depth to Proverbs, this Bible study represents only the high points. The goal for this study is to help you commit some of God's truths to memory and to whet your appetite for a life pursuit of wisdom.

—Ken Boa

As You Study

Spiritual maturity begins with a diligent study of the Word of God. The more you take in and live out, the more you grow in Christlikeness. There's no substitute for spending time in the Word. Time, however, is a diminishing resource in our complex society; and schedules are rarely routine for anyone.

To help address these issues, Dr. Boa and I have developed what we call the GUIDEBOOK series. Guided tours carry people to places of interest, providing information from experts along the way. People take guided tours for a number of reasons. Sometimes they don't know where to go. Sometimes they want more information. Sometimes their time is limited. Sometimes their understanding is limited. In all cases, they need a guidebook.

The GUIDEBOOK series is aptly named. The workbooks are vehicles and we (your tour guides) are longtime Bible teachers and writers. Dr. Boa, in fact, is a theological expert. As we guide you through Proverbs 1–9 we'll be drawing your attention to key verses within the book as well as to other related passages in Scripture. These passages are significant because of their relationship to something of greater importance; namely, God's plan of salvation.

To help you get the most out of your journey, read the suggestions in the adjacent column before you go on. We hope you'll enjoy *Pursuing Wisdom: A Biblical Approach from Proverbs.* Now, buckle your seat belt. We're ready to go!

—Gail Burnett

Getting the Most from Your Study

1. **Begin with prayer.** You can gain information on your own, but only God can reveal truth.

2. **Do not read commentaries on Proverbs until you have finished the entire study.** Self-discovery of biblical truth is exciting. It makes the Word of God come alive, and it also helps you retain what you've learned.

3. **Make sure you understand the structure of this GUIDEBOOK before you begin.** Explanations are found on page 7.

4. **Do not skip over directions to read the referenced Scriptures.** The text that follows may not make sense if you have not first read the Scripture passage(s).

5. **Be sure to write your answers to the study questions in the space provided.** Repetition and space for content interaction have been included to help you retain the material. Your answers will be confirmed in subsequent readings. These answers are intended to reinforce what you've already read and written.

6. **Work on this study every day of the week.** Begin the first day of your study week by reading the "unit introduction." Work through the Daily Excursions over the next five days, then end your week with review and Scripture memory. You may want to preview "Sharing the Journey" if you are using this study with a group.

7. **Read the articles and suggested Daily Readings in the optional Side Tours, even if you don't have time to do the activities.** The articles and readings are important, and they can be read in a few minutes.

8. **During your day, meditate on what you've learned.** Most Daily Excursions can be completed in less than twenty minutes, but they are "tightly packed." Reflecting on your observations allows biblical truths to expand your understanding and to take shape in your life.

How to Use This GuideBook

Instructional Design©

GuideBooks are self-contained, interactive Bible studies. These studies are primarily inductive; that is, they lead the reader to related Scriptures throughout the Bible so that he or she might experience the joy of self-discovery as revealed by the Master Himself. Therefore, in addition to Scripture references from the key texts, topics are supported by the whole counsel of God. Other outside material and additional Scripture references are included in "For further study."

Each GuideBook includes five study units divided into five **Daily Excursions**. Most Excursions take about twenty minutes to complete. No additional reference materials are needed. To complete the optional Side Tours, a Bible and a concordance are sometimes needed. Each unit ends with a session plan (Sharing the Journey) for group use in a Bible study, small group, or Sunday school class. (The leader will need to have a flipchart or board and markers or chalk available. All questions and activities should be adapted to best suit the needs of the group members.) While this section is intended for group use, you also can benefit from doing the activities on your own.

Page Description

GuideBooks are designed for open, two-page viewing. Each page is divided into two columns, a wide inside column and a narrow outside column, as shown below. Daily Excursions include Bible teaching, related questions, life application (Bringing It Home), and Bible reading. The outside columns contain related Road Map and Side Tour options. At the end of each unit, it is suggested that the reader select one verse from the weekly reading to memorize.

The **Road Map** includes all Bible verses referred to in the Daily Excursions, except for lengthy study texts. (These are provided in appendix A). Scriptures in the Road Map are linked to reference numbers in the Daily Excursions and numbered consecutively throughout the GuideBook. Unless otherwise noted, all Scripture passages are from the New American Standard Bible.

Within quoted Scriptures, **ellipses** (. . .) indicate where portions of text have been omitted (due to space constraints) without compromising the meaning. The verses provided include the essential information for your study; however, you will benefit from reading the full text from your Bible.

The **Side Tours** contain optional reading and Scripture references related to Language & Literature, History & Culture, Bible Study Techniques, Cross References, and Points of Interest (including life illustrations). All Side Tours are referenced in the text and numbered consecutively (preceded by "T") throughout the GuideBook. For example, the notation [T1] will follow the appropriate text in the Daily Excursion, and this same notation will appear in the adjacent Side Tour column. Because the Scriptures listed in Side Tours are not printed in this GuideBook, they must be looked up in a Bible.

Personal Experiences of the authors are differentiated by their names in parentheses.

ROAD MAP	DAILY EXCURSION	DAILY EXCURSION	SIDE TOURS

[1]PROVERBS 1
1 The proverbs [mashal] of Solomon the son of David, king of Israel:
2 To know wisdom and instruction, To discern the sayings of understanding,
3 To receive instruction in wise behavior, Righteousness, justice and equity;

DAY 1
EXAMINING PROVERBS AS LITERATURE

What defines a proverb? The Hebrew word for "proverb" is transliterated[T1] *mashal*, which means "a discourse or a parable." *Mashal* comes from a root word that means "to be similar or parallel; to represent; to be like or be compared to." The book of Proverbs uses comparisons as its primary literary device. A proverb may show how one

BRINGING IT HOME . . .
1. Look back at your life—as a child, a teen, and a young adult. Also look at your life now. At what point, if any, did you make a choice to reject being naive and foolish and to embrace wisdom? In what ways does that choice still impact your life today?

HISTORY & CULTURE:[T3]
AUTHORSHIP—King Solomon, son of David, did not write all of the proverbs, but his work makes up the greater part of the book. Solomon was an observer and a seeker of knowledge. Not only was Solomon's knowledge encyclopedic, his understanding and discernment were such that his wisdom was legendary. People

INTRODUCTION—THE STUDY OF PROVERBS

The book of Proverbs holds a central position in Scripture. As a book of wisdom literature (along with Job and Ecclesiastes), Proverbs exhorts, guides, and instructs us in the art of living. It shows us how to have a life of purpose and meaning by applying practical principles of holiness. This book deals with aspects of character and of living that are too fine to get caught in the mesh of the Law and too small to be addressed by the broad strokes of the Prophets.

The proverbs deal with the details of living where decisive elements of character are developed and exposed. They are practical, penetrating, and piercing; they're catchy and concise illustrations based on experiences common to us all. The proverbs are precepts or maxims that are easily memorized, applied, and understood—maxims that are backed up by universal principles with widely ranging applications.

A good definition of a proverb is this: *A simple illustration that exposes a fundamental reality about life.* A single proverb can speak volumes throughout history, with personal applications for every age and in every culture.

WHY STUDY PROVERBS?

The proverbs basically categorize all of humankind into two main people groups according to the thought processes and behaviors that distinguish one from the other: the wise and the foolish. Truly, we are like those described in the old Dutch proverb, "We grow too soon old and too late smart." Isn't it ironic that by the time we've learned wisdom from our own experience, our youth is spent? It takes time to gain perspective. It takes a lifetime, really, to learn the art of living. That's why the teachings of Proverbs are of infinite value to us. They offer wise counsel based on the collective experiences of those who have learned a fundamental truth worth passing on to future generations. Proverbs allow us to stand on the shoulders of giants so that we can see how to order our paths in the ways of the wise and thus avoid the consequences of wrong choices.

Those who learn and apply life's truths in advance are like mature drivers who are always looking far beyond the hood of the car, watching traffic patterns, and anticipating the actions of other drivers. Mature drivers plan their reactions to problems to include a margin of safety. They seldom wreck their cars. Likewise, a mature person is always looking far beyond his or her immediate circumstances, watching life patterns, discerning motives, and anticipating the actions of others. The principles and convictions of mature people are already in place, so when they face common temptations (power, sex, money) their integrity isn't compromised. And because they've predetermined how they will respond, mature people don't wreck their lives. They have simply "drawn the line" in advance—a line that includes a margin of moral safety.

That each of us will be tested is a given fact. But everything that happens, good and bad, can be an opportunity to grow and expand our perspective. If rightly analyzed and applied, even failure can become a tremendous learning experience. If not, failure can become a way of life. If we don't (or won't!) get the message, we'll get caught in destructive life patterns, doing the same foolish things over and over again, each time expecting different results. We'll use the same faulty logic but just vary the themes (get a new marriage partner or try a different get-rich scheme, for example). That's not maturity—that's insanity. Experience benefits only those who get the message.

In addition to learning from our own experiences, we need to learn from the experiences of others and to seek the counsel of those whose lives reflect wisdom. Someone said, "A wise man learns from the mistakes of others—nobody lives long enough to make them all himself." Ironically, we're often long on giving advice but short on listening to advice from others. In fact, we can be downright foolish when it comes to our own situations. Errors and absurdities are much more clearly seen in others than in ourselves—except, perhaps, in retrospect. In her poem "Wisdom," American poet Sara Teasdale wrote,

> When I have ceased to break my wings against the faultiness of things,
> And learned that compromises wait behind each hardly opened gate,
> When I can look life in the eyes, have grown calm and very coldly wise,
> Life will have given me the truth and taken in exchange, my youth.

With maturity, people are able to evaluate life. The patterns of the past become templates for shaping the present and anticipating the future. Actions and events become increasingly predictable so that a mature person can see further down the road and make wiser choices. This is a tremendous advantage, especially for the Christian. It's a mark of growth to confess and repent of our sins and learn something from our mistakes. It's greater and more beneficial, however, to read God's Word, listen to godly counsel, and do what is right in the first place. We have made great strides when we learn to turn away from temptation before our errors produce undesirable (and often irreversible) consequences.

The goal for studying Proverbs is to help us get beyond a habit of stumbling through life and past the heartache of recognizing "brick walls" only after we've crashed headlong into them. The world says, "You just gotta live and learn." But as recorded in Job 28, God makes His wisdom available to us (see selected verses in the adjacent column). And Wisdom shouts in all the avenues of life, *You don't have to just live and learn. You can learn from me . . . and live!*

JOB 28

12-18,20-21 But where can wisdom be found? And where is the place of understanding? Man does not know its value, nor is it found in the land of the living. The deep says, "It is not in me," and the sea says, "It is not with me." Pure gold cannot be given in exchange for it, nor can silver be weighed as its price. It cannot be valued in the gold of Ophir, in precious onyx, or sapphire. Gold or glass cannot equal it, . . . Coral and crystal are not to be mentioned; and the acquisition of wisdom is above that of pearls. . . . Where then does wisdom come from? And where is the place of understanding? Thus it is hidden from the eyes of all living, and concealed from the birds of the sky.

23-27 God understands its way; and He knows its place. For He looks to the ends of the earth, and sees everything under the heavens. When He imparted weight to the wind, and meted out the waters by measure, when He set a limit for the rain, and a course for the thunderbolt, then He saw it and declared it; He established it and also searched it out.

28 And to man He said, "Behold, the fear of the Lord, that is wisdom; and to depart from evil is understanding."

INTRODUCTION TO UNIT 1
AN OVERVIEW OF PROVERBS

Destination: To establish a historical, cultural, and literary framework for an in-depth study of Proverbs and a personal pursuit of wisdom.

The slow rocking of the front-porch chairs kept half-time to the mantle clock. Its loud ticking, clearly audible through the screen door, punctuated the dragging time—at least it seemed so to an impatient child. Five old uncles in bibbed overalls were comfortable with long stretches of silence. I (Gail) wasn't. But if I pouted, one of them would surely tell me, "Pick up your lower lip, child, or you'll someday trip over it."

Who knows why I remember so much of what little my uncles said. Perhaps it was because they were verbal misers. Perhaps it was the quaintness of their speech. More likely, however, it was the impact of their "old sayings"—sayings simple enough for a child to understand yet profound enough for a child to instinctively treasure. All I know is this: My Appalachian heritage, rich with those mountain maxims, has shaped my thinking as well as my speech.

Stop to consider words that have shaped your thinking and you find an amazing number of proverbs tucked into your childhood training. Your great grandmother said them, your grandmother and mother repeated them, and you've found (or will find) yourself passing them down to your children. Have you ever wondered how far back those sayings go? Who started them? Why?

Unit 1, "An Overview of Proverbs," will answer similar questions about this Old Testament book as a whole. *Who* wrote or collected these sayings? *Why* were these proverbs written or collected in the first place? *When?* For *whom* were these sayings intended? Within *what* historical and cultural context were they developed? *How* do they relate to and shape our lives today?

Some of you are just itching to find these answers. Others want to get right to the text and begin mining for the gems you know these Scriptures hold. Remember, however, that the best diamonds come from the deepest mines; and deep mining requires first building a shaft or a supportive framework. The answers to these questions provide the framework for our study—a structure that will be vital to understanding the text when we delve into this incredibly rich vein of God's truths. For this unit, focus on building your mine shaft. As you set your heart to diligently study, may you be like Ezra: "The good hand of his God was upon him. For Ezra had set his heart to study the law of the LORD, and to practice it, and to teach His statutes and ordinances in Israel" (Ezra 7:9-10).

EXAMINING PROVERBS AS LITERATURE

What defines a proverb? The Hebrew word for "proverb" is transliterated[T1] *mashal*, which means "a discourse or a parable." *Mashal* comes from a root word that means "to be similar or parallel; to represent; to be like or be compared to." The book of Proverbs uses comparisons as its primary literary device. A proverb may show how one principle is *like* something already known (synonymous parallel construction) or how another principle is *opposite* something already known (antithetical parallel construction).

Read Proverbs 1:1-7.¹ Verse 5 is an example of _____ parallel construction while verse 7 shows _____ parallel construction.

CHARACTERISTICS OF A PROVERB

Because proverbs are universal truths, they are found in the literature of all languages. A proverb has several characteristics that distinguish it from other types of literature. A proverb will be:

1. **Concise:** The English word is made up of *pro*, which means "for" and *verba*, which means "words." A proverb is a thought capsule; it's many words compressed into just a few.
2. **Clear:** A proverb will drive home a central point with great clarity. It will be sharp and piercing, hitting its target like a bullet.
3. **Complete:** With a few words, a proverb presents a single, stand-alone message with multiple applications.
4. **Catchy:** Proverbs are easy-to-remember, poetic[T2] phrases that create homey or earthy images. Proverbs speak of everyday experiences.
5. **Comparative:** Proverbs point to the similarities or differences within an issue or principle. (Proverbs 1:5 uses synonymous parallelism while Proverbs 1:7 uses antithetical parallel construction.)

DATE, LITERARY STRUCTURE, AND OUTLINE OF PROVERBS

The book of Proverbs was written or transcribed over a time period ranging from 931 to 700 B.C. The first nine chapters of Proverbs introduce wisdom and stress its immeasurable worth. These introductory chapters are intended to create a desire for the proverbial wisdom to follow in chapters 10–31.

Antithetical parallelism is primarily used in chapters 10–15. Typically, an image or concept is presented in the first line, and then its opposite (often introduced by "but" or "and") is contrasted in the second. Beginning with Proverbs 16:1 and continuing through 22:16, there's a sudden shift to *synonymous parallelism*. An image or concept is presented in the first line, and its likeness (often introduced by "like" or "as") is compared in the second.

Sayings of the wise begin in Proverbs 22:17 and continue through the end of chapter 24. A second collection of Solomon's proverbs are found in chapters 25–29. This second collection, which was translated during the reign of King Hezekiah some 230 years after Solomon's death, predominantly expands themes from Solomon's first collection. Two other men are mentioned as contributors to Proverbs. Agur is credited with the numerical proverbs from chapter 30, and King Lemuel claims authorship of the virtuous woman proverbs from chapter 31.

STUDY TECHNIQUE:[T1]

TRANSLITERATION—The original languages of the Scriptures—Hebrew/Aramaic (Old Testament) and Greek (New Testament)—do not use the English alphabet. Therefore, we must write these words phonetically (that is, we listen to how the Greek or Hebrew word sounds when it is spoken in its own language, then we spell out those sounds in English letters). The English phonetic spelling is called *transliteration*.

LANGUAGE & LIT:[T2]

HEBREW POETRY—Proverbs are an example of Hebrew poetry—a type of verse that rhymes ideas or concepts (not sounds) in either antithetical or synonymous parallels. Hebrew poetry is very subtle and metrical with a definite formula in the soul and rhythm.

COMING UP:
BRINGING IT HOME

Beginning on day 2, this study will include daily life application questions and activities.

²PROVERBS 1

²PROVERBS 1

1 The proverbs of Solomon the son of David, king of Israel:

2 To know wisdom and instruction, to discern the sayings of understanding,

3 To receive instruction in wise behavior, righteousness, justice and equity;

4 To give prudence to the naive, to the youth knowledge and discretion,

5 A wise man will hear and increase in learning, and a man of understanding will acquire wise counsel,

6 To understand a proverb and a figure, the words of the wise and their riddles.

DAY 2

LOOKING AT THE BIG PICTURE

We will be reading a portion of Proverbs each day so that by the end of this study, we will have read through all the introductory chapters. But today, we need to speed read Proverbs 1:1–8:36. Don't take more than twenty minutes, and don't be tempted to tarry at some fascinating juncture—just keep reading the high points! As you rapidly read, the theme of Proverbs will rise to the surface. When you have finished reading, write the main words that come to the forefront. (If you're still not sure, review Proverbs 1:1-6.²)

Proverbs is one of the few books that tells us right up front (verses 1-6) about its author and his purpose for writing. According to Proverbs 1:1, who is the primary author of Proverbs?[T3]

Proverbs 1:4-5 tells us something about the audience or recipients—those for whom the proverbs were written. These verses mention three different groups of people as the intended readers of the collection of proverbs. Who are they?

-
-
-

Read Proverbs 1:2-6 one more time. Meditate for a moment on the blessings of wisdom made available to the naive and the youth as well as to the wise man/man of understanding. Ask God to open your heart to receive instruction and wisdom as you exercise discipline in your study of Proverbs.

BRINGING IT HOME . . .

1. Look back at your life—as a child, a teen, and a young adult. Also look at your life now. At what point, if any, did you make a choice to reject being naive and foolish and to embrace wisdom? In what ways does that choice still impact your life today?

2. Ask God to reveal any area(s) in your life where you need to apply wisdom. Choose one area and write down how you can embrace wisdom.

3. Who or what has most influenced your desire for wisdom? In what ways? How are you influencing others in their pursuit of wisdom?

HISTORY & CULTURE:[T3]

AUTHORSHIP—King Solomon, son of David, did not write all of the proverbs, but his work makes up the greater part of the book. Solomon was an observer and a seeker of knowledge. Not only was Solomon's knowledge encyclopedic, his understanding and discernment were such that his wisdom was legendary. People would come hundreds of miles to hear him speak from his store of knowledge (on plants, animals, birds, and so on) and from his store of wisdom on life. Sadly, this wise man did not follow his own teachings. Because he failed to honor the Source of his wisdom, Solomon became foolish in his older years. Also written by Solomon, the book of Ecclesiastes shows an old man looking back at his own absurdities in sad reflection and repentance of earlier years.

For further study:
Who laid the foundation for Solomon's wisdom?
(1 Chronicles 22:5-13)
Why did God give Solomon wisdom?
(1 Kings 3:5-14)
How did Solomon's wisdom compare to the wisdom of others?
(1 Kings 4:29-34; 10:1-9)
What was Solomon's downfall?
(1 Kings 11:1-12)
Why was this a problem?
(Deuteronomy 17:14-20)

COMING UP:
DAILY BIBLE READING

This study includes daily reading of a portion of Proverbs, beginning on day 3 of this unit. These readings are provided in appendix A. By the end of this study, you will have read through the nine introductory chapters of the book of Proverbs.

Read prayerfully, for as you read, the Holy Spirit may highlight a verse or passage that will offer encouragement or deal with a particular issue in your life. You will be asked to mark the verse that stands out most to you in each day's reading. At the end of the unit, you will want to select one of those verses to memorize.

DAY 3

UNDERSTANDING KEY WORDS AND CONCEPTS

³PROVERBS 1

2-6 To know wisdom [chokmah] and instruction, to discern the sayings of understanding,

To receive instruction [musar] in wise behavior, righteousness, justice and equity;

To give prudence to the naive, to the youth knowledge and discretion,

A wise man will hear and increase in learning, and a man of understanding will acquire wise counsel,

To understand a proverb and a figure, the words of the wise and their riddles.

On day 1, you discovered that most of the proverbs were written or collected by Solomon, son of David, king of Israel. Solomon's purpose was to instruct the naive, the youth, and the wise men in knowledge, understanding, discernment, and prudence so that they might live lives of righteousness, justice, equity, knowledge, and discretion. This, in essence, is what the whole collection of proverbs is about: the value of wisdom and instruction and the consequences of wise and foolish behavior. Because the words "wisdom," "instruction," and "fools" (or "the foolish") are woven throughout the entire book of Proverbs, let's look at each of these key words in more detail.

- **Wisdom** in the Hebrew language is transliterated *chokmah,* a word that carries the idea of gaining skill. In Proverbs, this skill is in the art of living a life endowed with the wisdom of God. The wisdom of Proverbs relates to moral acumen, practical righteousness, and integrity. It incorporates a spiritual component that enables us to think through our decisions with insight and to react with discipline. Wisdom is much more than intellect (though intelligence is a by-product). *The wisdom of Proverbs is the application of knowledge and truth to our daily lives.*

- **Instruction** in Hebrew is transliterated *musar,* which means "to discipline, to correct." This word's link with the word "wisdom" tells us that acquiring skill in the art of living will require discipline and diligence.

- **Fools** or **the foolish** in Proverbs are translated from four different Hebrew words that differentiate groups of people according to their degrees of foolishness. Proverbs reveals a gallery of fools, beginning with the naive and progressing downward to the scoffer. (We'll be discussing each type of fool in unit 2.)

LOST IN THE TRANSLATION

Before taking a foreign language, I (Gail) used to think that for every word in any foreign dictionary, there was an equivalent English word and vice versa. It never occurred to me that some concepts common to my experience did not even exist in other languages (try explaining "computer" in some third-world countries). I also didn't realize that beyond the strictest definition, words can carry ideas or symbolisms unique to a culture.

In Scripture, God has seen to it that His message of salvation is clear, both across cultures and across time. But we often miss the nuances or the richness of some passages because the symbolism or "cultural baggage" is lost in the translations.[T4] Read through Proverbs 1:2-6[3] again. What are the actions (verbs) and related benefits? In the chart below, list each of the verb infinitives (preceded by "to") and the benefits associated with each one. (The first one is done for you as an example.)

Verbs	Benefits
■ *to know*	■ *wisdom and instruction*
■	■
■	■
■	■
■	■

EXAMPLE OF CONCORDANCE AND DICTIONARY ENTRIES

MAIN CONCORDANCE

English word —

Scripture location —

Numbers keyed to Hebrew/Aramaic or Greek dictionary

WISE
tree to be desired to make one *w* .... Gen 3:6 7919
Egypt, and all the *w* men thereof .... Gen 41:8 2450

As used in the KJV —

and the foolish said to the *w* .... Mt 25:8 5429

GREEK DICTIONARY

Number key in Greek dictionary   *Greek spelling*   *Transliteration (English phonetic spelling)*   *Root word*

5429. φρουιμοδ **phronimos** *fron'-ee-mos;* from *5424;* i.e., *thoughtful, i.e. sagacious or discreet* (implying a *cautious* character; while *4680* denotes *practical* skill or acumen; and *4908* indicates rather *intelligence* or mental acquirement); in a bad sense *conceited* (also in the compar.): —wise (-r).

WORD STUDIES—Word studies are a basic and simple technique that can shed tremendous light on a biblical passage. Translation isn't an easy task. Denotations (simple definitions) may translate fairly easily from one language to another, but connotations (cultural baggage) may not. It is helpful, therefore, to examine a word in its original language to get a better understanding of its full meaning.

We look up repeated words or concepts (in their language of origin) because these are always key to understanding the text. There are many books, study Bibles, and computer programs that make word studies a simple process. One easy-to-use study tool is a concordance. Each English word is assigned a number that is keyed to a Hebrew/Aramaic or Greek dictionary supplied in the back of the concordance. These dictionaries include the word's meaning and root word (from which the word of interest was derived).

Concordances are based on particular Bible versions. A well-known one using the King James Version is *Strong's Exhaustive Concordance*. This study is based on the New American Standard Bible. The *New American Standard Exhaustive Concordance of the Bible* is published by Holman Bible Publishers.

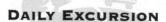
⁴PROVERBS 1

7 The fear of the LORD is the beginning of knowledge; Fools despise wisdom and instruction.

Isn't the list of benefits impressive! Who wouldn't want to discern wise sayings, to be prudent and discrete, to know how to behave wisely, to increase in learning—even to be able to figure out riddles? But doesn't our English verb list seem a little passive or bland by comparison to these powerful character traits? That's because the energy and intensity of these verbs are somewhat muted by translation. Look at these verbs in the Hebrew:

- To know, *yada:* to acknowledge; to clearly understand; to know with certainty

- To discern/understand, *bin:* to diligently consider; to investigate

- To receive, *laqach:* to capture; to seize

- To give, *nathan:* to apportion; to ascribe; to commit; to assign

The Hebrew meanings suggest that attaining these benefits will involve a much more intensive, aggressive engaging of our minds, wills, and spirits than the English verbs might lead us to believe. *Gaining wisdom requires that we be wholly, fully, and actively involved in its pursuit.*

Read Proverbs 1:2³ again. Here wisdom includes the development of moral awareness and discretion (discerning right and wrong) as well as mental or intellectual abilities. Note that the wisdom seeker must be willing to *receive* instruction. This won't be easy. To the Hebrew, the meaning of instruction *(musar)* encompassed admonishment, correction, discipline, reproof, warning—even chastening! *Gaining wisdom also requires, then, that we be wholly and continuously teachable.*

KEY VERSE

Along with author, audience, and purpose, the key verse in Proverbs is also found up front. Read Proverbs 1:7.⁴ This verse says that the fear of God—a sense of God's holiness and righteousness; an awe of God—is the beginning of knowledge. God's blueprint for living is revealed in Proverbs, but if we are not in awe of God, we will not order our paths in ways that are compatible with His will. Write the key verse on a three- by five-inch index card, then commit it to memory.ᵀ⁵

BRINGING IT HOME . . .

1. Review the verbs from Proverbs 1:2-6 on page 16. Are you actively pursuing wisdom? What action will you take today to internalize wisdom from God? What about tomorrow?

2. Are your principles of Christian doctrine based on childhood teachings alone or have they been reinforced with a personal study of God's Word? Are you teachable? Or do you turn a deaf ear to Scriptures that don't line up with your belief system? Rate your teachability on a scale of 1 to 10 (with 10 being "very teachable"). Ask someone close to you to also rate your teachability, then compare the scores.

3. In what areas does society entice you personally to sin? What are you doing (or can you do) to avoid following the crowd? Ask God to show you one specific change you can make to strengthen your stand against evil.

STUDY TECHNIQUE:[T5]
TIPS FOR SCRIPTURE MEMORY—Whatever we're consistently exposed to eventually imprints on our minds—even when we don't want it to. The hard part of memorizing isn't the retention, it's the discipline to review the material until it sticks. Try this Scripture memory technique: Write your selected verse (with book/chapter/verse) on a three- by five-inch index card and post it wherever you will encounter it most often. Each time you see it, read it three times until you can say it from memory before falling asleep and again before rising. Each week start a new verse and review the old cards so the Scriptures won't fade from memory!

DAILY READING
Read Proverbs 1:1-7. Mark the proverb that stands out most to you today.

[5]**EXODUS 28**

2-3 "And you shall make holy garments for Aaron your brother, for glory and for beauty. And you shall speak to all the skillful persons whom I [God] have endowed with the spirit of wisdom, that they make Aaron's garments to consecrate him, that he may minister as priest to Me."

[6]**EXODUS 31**

1-6 Now the LORD spoke to Moses, saying, "See, I have called by name Bezalel, . . . And I have filled him with the Spirit of God in wisdom, in understanding, in knowledge, and in all kinds of craftsmanship, to make artistic designs for work in gold, in silver, and in bronze, and in the cutting of stones for settings, and in the carving of wood, that he may work in all kinds of craftsmanship. And behold, I Myself have appointed with him Oholiab, . . . and in the hearts of all who are skillful I have put skill, that they may make all that I have commanded you."

[7]**EXODUS 35**

34 He also has put in his [Bezalel's] heart to teach, both he and Oholiab, the son of Ahisamach, of the tribe of Dan.

DAY 4

RELATING WISDOM TO SKILL

On day 3 we learned that the Hebrew word for "wisdom" (*chokmah*) relates to developing a skill. We discovered this relationship, in part, by looking at the word(s) from which *chokmah* was derived; that is, the root word(s). *Chokmah* comes from the root word *chakam*, a word whose meaning includes both "to be wise" and "to behave wisely."

We also looked at the word "wisdom" as it is used in other *contexts*,[T6] particularly where it first appears in Scripture (this is called the *principle of first mention*[T7]). We found that the words "wisdom" and "skill," or the mention of a specific skill, are often linked together in related Scripture. "Skillful" appears in the same verse where "wisdom" is first mentioned, and it is translated from the same Hebrew word as the root word for wisdom—*chakam*. Moreover, in other texts, *chakam* is translated "wise; expert; sage." From these two word study techniques we were able to see a fundamental link between wisdom and skill.

Wisdom is first mentioned in Exodus 28:3. The larger context is this: Moses is consecrating the priesthood and supervising the construction of the tabernacle in the wilderness. Read Exodus 28:2-3[5] (verse 2 provides the immediate context), then answer the following questions.

What was to be made that required skill?

What two characteristics should this item reflect?
-
-

From whom do the workers get skill to complete their assignments?

There are other Scriptures that reveal insights on the source of wisdom and on wisdom's relationship to attaining a skill. In Exodus 28:2-3, God supplied skill and wisdom through His Spirit to make the holy garments. These garments were important because they would serve as types and shadows (physical representations or pictures) of what would become a spiritual reality in Christ, reflecting His glory and beauty.[T8]

Read Exodus 31:1-6.[6] Bezalel was anointed in what four areas?

-
-
-
-

Again, from what source did Bezalel get his skills and wisdom?

One might get the impression that God suddenly zapped Bezalel, Oholiab, and others with skill and wisdom right on the spot! But there's a clue in Exodus 35 that suggests this was not the case. According to Exodus 35:34,[7] what was "also" put in the hearts of these men?

The making of human teachers infers the existence of those who must be taught. But if instant wisdom had been endowed on Bezalel and Oholiab, why not on everyone else as needed? Why waste time teaching and learning? It seems, then, that "a heart to teach" might preclude ideas of instant and out-of-the-blue wisdom. This doesn't mean that God's power is limited. He certainly *could* (and may) grant instant knowledge in some needed circumstance. But throughout Scripture, and particularly in Proverbs, God calls us to a diligent and disciplined pursuit of knowledge and wisdom.

STUDY TECHNIQUE:[T6]
CONTEXT—When interpreting the meaning of Scripture passages, context rules. If out of the blue I were to say "fish," would I be talking about a sport, a sea creature, a card game, or bait for a compliment? But if I were holding a pole, you could safely conclude "sport" by the visual *context*. Context in Scripture refers to the bigger picture or vision surrounding a word, verse, chapter, or book of the Bible. The broader context includes the history, culture, time, setting, government, circumstances, and so on that influenced the writing or the author. The more immediate context includes the verses, subjects, key words, concepts, and doctrinal issues that surround the verses of interest.

STUDY TECHNIQUE:[T7]
PRINCIPLE OF FIRST MENTION—One way to gain insight on a word's fuller meaning is to look at the context surrounding the first time that word is introduced in Scripture. Sometimes we are surprised. Love, for example, is not mentioned first of Adam toward Eve but of Abraham toward Isaac. God said, "take your only son, whom you love . . ." to be sacrificed. Love's first mention was the foreshadowing of the greatest act of love the world would ever know—God's gift of His Son. The full expression of any text can be found *only* within the whole of the idea being presented. This is why context is critical to correct interpretation of Scripture.

[8]**2 TIMOTHY 2**

15 Be diligent to present yourself approved to God as a workman who does not need to be ashamed, handling accurately the word of truth.

[9]**2 PETER 1**

5-8,10 Now for this very reason also, applying all diligence, in your faith supply moral excellence, and in your moral excellence, knowledge; and in your knowledge, self-control, and in your self-control, perseverance, and in your perseverance, godliness; and in your godliness, brotherly kindness, and in your brotherly kindness, love. For if these qualities are yours and are increasing, they render you neither useless nor unfruitful in the true knowledge of our Lord Jesus Christ. . . . Therefore, brethren, be all the more diligent to make certain about His calling and choosing you; for as long as you practice these things, you will never stumble.

[10]**JEREMIAH 29**

13-14 "And you will seek Me and find Me, when you search for Me with all your heart.

"And I will be found by you," declares the LORD.

Read 2 Timothy 2:15[8] and 2 Peter 1:5-8,10.[9]

These Scriptures (along with Proverbs) support what may seem like a paradox. On the one hand, if we would be wise, we must apply ourselves toward that end. On the other hand, all our efforts toward achieving wisdom are really fruitless; it ultimately rests on the work of God through His Spirit. Perhaps this paradox could be resolved by reading Jeremiah 29:13-14.[10]

In verse 13, who does the seeking?

Note how the subject (the one doing the action) changes in verse 14. We could never "find" God by looking for Him. Who takes the responsibility for our finding God?

How might the verses in Jeremiah resolve our seeming paradox; namely, that we must actively pursue a wisdom that none can ever attain because it must be endowed by God?

God's eye is ever upon us, and He meets us at the point of our obedience. When we truly desire Him, we will seek Him. When we seek Him, He comes to us, fulfilling the deepest longings of our heart with Himself.

Now let's go back to the skills of Bezalel, Oholiab, and others. If these people were not "zapped" with abilities, then when or where did the workers get their wilderness skills? How were they able to create such exquisite items for the tabernacle? Would it be any less a miracle if a sovereign (all-powerful) and omniscient (all-knowing) God had gifted Bezalel, Oholiab, and all the skillful workers with the appropriate raw material from birth? And would it be any less amazing if back in Egypt He had directed each person into those areas of work to prepare them for their most important life assignment? And would it require any less of God for even talented and skillful people to produce something exquisite in the wilderness that was "exceeding abundantly beyond all that we ask or think" (Ephesians 3:20)?

Do you ever wonder what you are doing now that God wants one day to use mightily for His purposes? (By the way, do you know how these poor, ex-slaves in the desert got such lavish raw materials to work with?[T9])

BRINGING IT HOME . . .

1. Think about how well you apply yourself to your job at work, your ministry at church, or your work at home. If an objective, outside observer were to evaluate your normal performance in these areas (job, church, home), which of the following phrases would this person use?

   ▪ Exceeds expectations

   ▪ Meets expectations

   ▪ Does not meet expectations

   Seek God's insight and evaluation in each area. What changes can you make to improve your performance? Write them down and then commit them to the Lord.

2. What special skills and abilities has God given you? In what ways, if any, are you using these skills for kingdom work? Ask God to show you where He wants you to serve. Ask your pastor or others at church where your abilities can best be used.

HISTORY & CULTURE:[T8]

THE TABERNACLE —With the giving of the Law, the priesthood, the sacrifices, the feasts, and the rituals, God instituted His own rules of order and worship. The tabernacle was the mobile place of worship built under the direction of God through Moses when the children of Israel were in the wilderness. Exodus 25–40 details the tabernacle and furnishings.

The tabernacle and furnishings are a magnificent physical representation of a coming spiritual reality in Christ. Read Exodus 25:8-9 and 26:30. The tabernacle had only one entrance (see John 10:7-9), a golden lampstand (see John 8:12), an altar for the sin sacrifice (see John 1:29), a table of unleavened bread (see John 6:32-35), and an altar of incense (see Revelation 5:8 and 8:3-4). Now, carefully read Hebrews 9:1-14, 10:14-20, and Matthew 27:50-51. What an awesome God!

HISTORY & CULTURE:[T9]

GOLD IN THE DESERT—Have you ever wondered where a nation of slaves got gold and fine linen for the tabernacle—in the middle of the desert? The answer is found in Exodus 12:29-36. At first these verses can be puzzling. What God told Israel to do seemed dishonest! Now read Exodus 1:1-14 in light of Jeremiah 22:13, Malachi 3:5-6, and Psalm 50:11-12. You know, for both those whose wages are withheld and those who selfishly withhold, it truly will be "pay day, some day." Are you fairly dividing the riches God is *lending* you with those whose labors are producing your wealth?

DAILY READING

Read Proverbs 1:8-19. Mark the proverb that stands out most to you today.

DAY 5

LEARNING DISCIPLINE: THE PATH TO FREEDOM

[11] JOB 5

17 Behold, how happy is the man whom God reproves, so do not despise the discipline of the Almighty.

[12] PSALM 119

67,71 Before I was afflicted I went astray, but now I keep Thy word.

It is good for me that I was afflicted, that I may learn Thy statutes.

[13] REVELATION 3

19 "Those whom I love, I reprove and discipline; be zealous therefore, and repent."

Our culture has some strange and negative notions about discipline. Many view it as punishment; and indeed, we cannot always differentiate between the two based on observed behaviors or actions. Suppose, for example, you were unusually busy this week and didn't finish all of your Bible study preparation. If, on the night before group time, you turn off the television to study, would you be exercising discipline or inflicting self-punishment? The defining factor is this: Motive! Punishment points out our guilt and demands payment. Discipline protects us *from* guilt and commands growth. If your motive is "correction toward perfection," you're exercising the self-discipline necessary to learn. Similarly, when God (not sin) brings us to a difficult place that fosters personal growth and spiritual maturity, He is not punishing us but developing us through divine discipline.

Discipline is also the bridge that spans the chasm between chaos and creativity, bondage and freedom. Let me (Ken) illustrate this principle. Sometimes when I'm listening to someone play the piano, I close my eyes and imagine that I am playing it myself. I think, *Wouldn't it be great if I could just sit down and have the freedom to do that?* The fact is, I *do* have the freedom to sit down at a piano and hit the keys. But even if I were blessed with raw talent, I would not be free to create beautiful music apart from the discipline required to both learn and improve. Without discipline, I will remain in bondage to musical chaos.

The finest musicians know they must be disciplined. They must continue to practice the basics while ever stretching to add to their musical skills. Like playing an instrument, wisdom also is attained by discipline and practice. We, too, must learn and stretch to add to our life skills while continuing to practice the basics we already know. If we submit to God's rule and dominion and allow Him to shape us, He will make our lives into something beautiful. God Himself will teach us, make our lives pleasing to Him, and bring us freedom.[T10]

Read Job 5:17[11] and Psalm 119:67,71.[12] How should we react to God's reproof?

Look at Revelation 3:19.[13] Who does God discipline?

Even in the most foundational sense, the wisdom gained by discipline is the path to freedom. Proverbs will tell us that wisdom rejects the invitation of crime, provides a sense of security and safety, keeps us financially solvent, enriches our relationships, protects us from elicit sensuality and its consequences, and keeps us from being foolish and lazy. Look at this list in the negative. People who are not wise invoke upon themselves imprisonment, financial ruin, broken relationships, disease and disappointments from sexual improprieties, embarrassment and loss from foolish behavior, and an overall unproductive life. It's not discipline, but the lack of discipline, that puts us into bondage. Self-discipline will serve us well, but God's discipline will set us free!

PASSING ON TRUTH

Ecclesiastes 12:9-11 provides us with a picture of the wise as referred to in Proverbs 22:1, namely, the *chakamin*.

> In addition to being a wise man, the Preacher [*qoheleth*] also taught the people knowledge; and he pondered, searched out, and arranged many proverbs. The Preacher sought to find delightful words and to write words of truth correctly. The words of wise men are like goads, and masters of *these* collections are like well-driven nails; they are given by one Shepherd.

In addition to the priests who imparted the Law and the prophets who communicated divine words and visions, Israel had sages or elders who gave counsel to the people, provided practical instruction, and taught schools of wisdom—an institution that has virtually vanished today!

Solomon, the Preacher (the *qoheleth*, "a collector of sayings"), and Hezekiah were both godly kings who desired to help the people learn the art of skillful living. In those days, words of wisdom were treasured and documented. People actively sought out the wise to learn from them. In fact, people went around swapping proverbs (thus some are similar to the wisdom writings of Amenemope of Egypt dated from 1000 to 600 B.C.).

POINT OF INTEREST:[T10]
SKILL AND DISCIPLINE—
The process of developing a skill requires discipline. And while discipline is not punishment, it still is not an easy thing to go through. The process of taking raw material and shaping it into something beautiful can be painful, but God is a master artisan.

We come into the world as raw material—spiritually and intellectually "formless and void." We must be developed under the instruction of the Word. Like silver in the hands of a master craftsman, so are our lives in the hands of a loving God. His skilled hands will shape our lives, refining us as silver for the art of living. It is God's discipline that enables us to evolve into greater Christlikeness "from glory to glory."

For further study:
Zechariah 13:9
Hebrews 12:5-11

[14] ISAIAH 58

12 And those from among you will rebuild the ancient ruins; You will raise up the age-old foundations; And you will be called the repairer of the breach, the restorer of the streets in which to dwell.

[15] PSALM 78

1-8 Listen, O my people, to my instruction; Incline your ears to the words of my mouth. I will open my mouth in a parable; I will utter dark sayings of old, which we have heard and known, and our fathers have told us. We will not conceal them from their children, but tell to the generation to come the praises of the LORD, and His strength and His wondrous works that He has done.

For He established a testimony in Jacob, and appointed a law in Israel, which He commanded our fathers, that they should teach them to their children, that the generation to come might know, even the children yet to be born, that they may arise and tell them to their children, that they should put their confidence in God, and not forget the works of God, but keep His commandments, and not be like their fathers, a stubborn and rebellious generation, a generation that did not prepare its heart, and whose spirit was not faithful to God.

The most fundamental resource in Israel for teaching the words of wisdom, however, was the elderly. Though not in a formal system, grandparents and parents taught their children. Elders in a family were revered for their wisdom; and in everyday settings, they assumed responsibilities for transferring their knowledge and insights to the young. How does this compare to our contemporary society?

Many of us missed out on having wise instruction passed down to us by our parents and grandparents. Unfortunately, when a generation or two fails to teach, it creates a gap or breach in the flow of wisdom; the ball is dropped for future generations.

The good news is that through God's Word, we can stand in the gap (or the breach) and start the ball rolling again as a blessing to our children and to our children's children. Read Isaiah 58:12.[14]

Beginning with our own generation, we can be disciplined to receive instruction and to develop skill in the art of living—learning the wisdom of God for ourselves and teaching it to the generations that follow. We must also reach beyond our own children and invest in other little hearts open to receiving wisdom from their elders. Read Psalm 78:1-8[15] and answer the following questions.

What is the speaker about to utter?

Where did these sayings come from?

To whom is he about to tell these sayings?

Specifically, which family member did God command to teach the children?

What was each generation's responsibility?

The Scriptures are clear in their admonishment to teach God's truths to our children and our children's children.[T11] Read the following verses from Deuteronomy.

4:9-10: Only give heed to yourself and keep your soul diligently, lest you forget the things which your eyes have seen, and lest they depart from your heart all the days of your life; but make them known to your sons and your grandsons. Remember the day you stood before the LORD your God at Horeb, when the LORD said to me, "Assemble the people to Me, that I may let them hear My words so they may learn to fear Me all the days they live on the earth, and that they may teach their children."

6:1-2,6-7: Now this is the commandment, the statutes and the judgments which the LORD your God has commanded me to teach you, that you might do them in the land where you are going over to possess it, so that you and your son and your grandson might fear the LORD your God, to keep all His statutes and His commandments, which I command you, all the days of your life, and that your days may be prolonged. . . . And these words, which I am commanding you today, shall be on your heart; and you shall teach them diligently to your sons and shall talk of them when you sit in your house and when you walk by the way and when you lie down and when you rise up.

List the activities from Deuteronomy 6 that define when this diligent teaching should take place.

-
-
-

BRINGING IT HOME . . .

1. What are some stories from your life (or the lives of your parents or grandparents) you can use to impart wisdom to future generations? Record at least one story and the truth it imparts.

2. If you are a father, in what ways are you taking the lead in teaching your children God's wisdom? Remember that change takes place one step at a time. If you are a mother, in what ways are you affirming your husband in his teaching role? In what ways can you teach your children about wisdom?

POINT OF INTEREST:[T11]
KIDS AND GRANDPARENTS—
As I (Ken) reflect on my own life, I recognize how profitable it was for me when I was under the tutelage of my grandparents, especially my grandmother. I spent a lot of time with her and with my two grandfathers also (but not as much time as I would have liked). I vividly remember many times when one grandfather or the other would deliberately set me down not only to tell me stories, but also to communicate wisdom through those stories. My grandfathers' stories always had meaning behind them— they weren't arbitrary tales.

It's tragic that many children don't have nurturing contacts with the elderly. Not only is this a loss for both the young and the elderly, it's a loss for our culture as well. Isn't our society now reaping the results from neglecting to teach wisdom and morals to its youth? May God give us more opportunities. May we respond in wisdom.

DAILY READING
Read Proverbs 1:20-33 and mark the proverb that stands out most to you today. Review all the proverbs you've marked over this five-day study and select one to commit to memory.

To the leader: For this session, have a few examples of modern-day proverbs displayed on the board or flip chart.

Write down a modern-day proverb and share it with the group. Ask how many people have heard it.

1. We have learned that a proverb is a concise, clear, complete, catchy comparison that exposes a fundamental reality about life.
   - Read Proverbs 1:1-7. How do the proverbs we've just compiled compare to the wisdom spoken of in these verses?
   - What famous American was known for his "proverbs"?
   - Who is well-known today for his or her proverbial wisdom?

2. In spite of his remarkable, God-given wisdom, Solomon failed to heed his own advice and experienced the painful outcomes that his proverbs predicted. Share examples of someone who violated the very counsel he or she gave to others.
   - What was the result of this inconsistency between this person's talk and walk?
   - How do people get so far off track? (Look at Deuteronomy 17:14-20 and 1 Kings 11:1-12 for some ideas.)

3. A number of people in the American public sector are known for their superior intellect. A few may be known for their (relative) ethics or morals. However, virtually no American public figure is famous for his or her wisdom. Our current culture tends to elevate the most foolish among us—especially in entertainment. In contrast, the ancients gave status to the wise whose sayings and writings (proverbs) were actually a kind of commodity that could be traded and treasured.
   - Why do you think there has been such a shift in how wisdom is valued and appreciated in our modern culture?
   - How can Christians reverse this trend both at home and in the church?

4. The wisdom of Old Testament Scriptures relates to developing a skill needed for living life to its fullest.
   - Share an example of when you sought, received, and heeded wise counsel. Make sure to include who gave that counsel and how it contributed to the quality of your life. Also mention how and when you have passed on (or plan to pass on) this wisdom to others.
   - For what decision or concern in your life right now do you need to seek wise counsel?
   - Who might be a good source of this counsel? (As each person shares, brainstorm additional ideas of where he or she might go for input. Remember: This is not a time to give advice. Just share possible resources.)

5. Day 5 of this week's study focused on discipline as the path to freedom. This almost sounds like an oxymoron or contradiction in terms.
   - How has this principle been revealed in your own life? In the lives of others?
   - For each of the settings listed below, give examples of discipline and the freedom it can lead to.

	Discipline	Freedom
Home		
Church		
Work		
School		
Sports		

   - How does discipline differ from punishment? Give specific examples for the settings listed above.

Close your group time with prayer for group members to be open and responsive to God's instruction so they may avoid His discipline. Also ask God to help you learn from His discipline.

INTRODUCTION TO UNIT 2
EXAMINING PROVERBS 1:7

Destination: To gain an understanding of the relationships among the fear of God, the knowledge of truth, and the wisdom of God.

As an engineering student at Case Institute of Technology, I (Ken) spent many hours working on calculus problems that would employ a single theorem. The professor would give us an engineering dilemma, and we would "solve" for what seemed an eternity. Instead of moving us on to a new theorem, however, the professor would just assign a different application of the same one until we were able to apply it to many types of engineering problems. He knew that until we mastered a foundational understanding, we would never be able to grasp the advanced concepts that awaited us in higher-level courses.

Unit 2 deals with a foundational "theorem" found in the key verse, "The fear of the LORD is the beginning of knowledge; Fools despise wisdom and instruction" (Proverbs 1:7). All five days of study will be dedicated to this key verse. After this unit, we will be studying much larger portions of texts. However, if you master this verse, you will be able to handle the material to follow.

The focus of this unit is to examine the relationships among the fear of God, the knowledge of truth, and the wisdom of God. As you study, you should become more aware of the importance of yielding control to the only One who truly has control. This can be very liberating! Making decisions independently of God is dangerous guesswork. It's like driving sixty miles per hour at night with your headlights shining straight down. God alone has all the facts, and He alone knows the future. Looking ahead, He gives us signs along the road of life, preparing us for the curves ahead, usually through Scripture.

Even when Scripture doesn't speak directly to our circumstances, God still speaks to our hearts through His Spirit. God's Spirit may instruct us in ways that conflict with what our senses or circumstances tell us (but *never* conflict with Scripture). If we know God's character, we can trust His direction over our own senses. Like a pilot who, at zero visibility, trusts his instrument panel over his own judgment, we too must trust God and rest in His guiding instruments—His Word, His church, and His Spirit.

As you begin this unit, ask God for the ability to yield control of your life to Him. Ask also for a new revelation of Himself.

DAY 1

BECOMING WISE

[16]**JEREMIAH 8**

9 "The wise men are put to shame, They are dismayed and caught; Behold, they have rejected the word of the LORD, And what kind of wisdom do they have?"

[17]**1 CORINTHIANS 1**

19-20 For it is written, "I WILL DESTROY THE WISDOM OF THE WISE, AND THE CLEVERNESS OF THE CLEVER I WILL SET ASIDE." Where is the wise man? Where is the scribe? Where is the debater of this age? Has not God made foolish the wisdom of the world?

[18]**1 CORINTHIANS 3**

18-21 Let no man deceive himself. If any man among you thinks that he is wise in this age, let him become foolish that he may become wise. For the wisdom of this world is foolishness before God. For it is written, "HE IS THE ONE WHO CATCHES THE WISE IN THEIR CRAFTINESS;" and again, "THE LORD KNOWS THE REASONINGS OF THE WISE, THAT THEY ARE USELESS." So then let no one boast in men.

In unit 1, we learned about the author of the first collection of proverbs and discovered an appropriate title: *The Proverbs of Solomon*. We also learned that proverbs were written to three specific groups of people (recipients or audience). Do you recall the first two groups in Proverbs 1:4?[1]

■

■

All young people are naive, but not all naive people are young. The *naive* and the *youth* in Proverbs 1:4 represent two groups of people that lack learning by reason of age or opportunity. They may either have been unexposed to truth or unable to comprehend truth—*but they haven't yet rejected truth*. Theirs is a temporary condition, for they must eventually either accept the truths of God and become increasingly wise or reject the truths of God and become increasingly foolish. (We'll look at this more on day 5.)

Do you agree or disagree with each of these statements? Why, or why not?

	Agree	Disagree	
1.	☐	☐	Formal education makes one wise.
2.	☐	☐	All wise people are intelligent.
3.	☐	☐	All intelligent people are wise.
4.	☐	☐	The wise person never stops learning.

A third group for whom the proverbs were intended is mentioned in Proverbs 1:5.[1] This group encompasses men of two characteristics, namely:

■

■

What are the habitual behaviors of this group?

■

■

The Hebrew word(s) for wise is translated in other Scripture passages as "the skillful, the shrewd, the sage, or the expert." The Hebrew word(s) for "men of understanding" appears in other portions of Scripture as "the clever, the intelligent, and the observant." The intellect of the wise may involve formal education or may be independent of it, for those who *understand* simply are those who diligently consider, gaze into, observe, perceive, and ponder. They are "knowing" because, formally or informally, they have pursued (and keep pursuing) truth.

The "wise man" and "the man of understanding" may appear to represent different groups of people—the first, "smart" men and the second, men "of great insight." But the habits that define men of understanding are the same habits that develop men of wisdom. The person rightly related to God—the one who observes, ponders, and asks God for insight—will be granted *un*common sense. Therefore, the wise man (the sage) and the man of understanding (the seeker of knowledge) illustrate stages of growth inherent in each person pursuing the knowledge of God.

The more important point of Proverbs 1:5 is that the distinguishing mark of the wise is their *continued* pursuit of knowledge and understanding. The already wise will continue to study wisdom literature (primarily Scripture) and will continue to seek wise counsel. Why? Because the more they comprehend God's infinite knowledge and perceive God's unfathomable wisdom, the less they will want to rely on personal faulty judgments.[T12] No matter how wise one becomes, his or her wisdom remains wholly dependent upon divine insight—upon God's revelation of truth.

All wise people are intelligent, but not all intelligent people are wise. Read Jeremiah 8:9[16] and 1 Corinthians 1:19-20[17] and 3:18-21.[18] What happens when the wisdom of the world is held up "before God"?

What does the Lord call the "reasonings of the [worldly] wise?"

HISTORY & CULTURE:[T12]

GATHERING DATA vs. GAINING WISDOM—The ancients, both Jew and Gentile, were seekers of wisdom. Today we are seekers of information (data or facts). Information can lead to knowledge and knowledge can lead to wisdom. But education in our generation seems to stop the process short of its ultimate goal. Rather than encourage wisdom, university educators in our culture equip us for the folly of autonomy; that is, the idea that we are self-sufficient and that we can order our own paths and do whatever we'd like.

Proverbs teaches a different message. God Himself may strip us of our self-sufficiency to clothe us in His all-sufficiency. He may allow us to flounder in our own areas of expertise until we feel we've lost control. He wants to teach us that we never were in control and never will be. This is an important lesson to learn because believing we are in control and holding to the delusion of self-sufficiency are at the very core of most anxieties that affect humankind.

For further study:
Can you control your business? (James 4:13)
Can you control your own prosperity? (Haggai 1:5-11)
Can you control your ministry? (John 15:4-5)
What does God say about human anxiety? (Matthew 6:25-34)

¹⁹JEREMIAH 50

6 "My people have become lost sheep; Their shepherds have led them astray."

²⁰MATTHEW 9

36 And seeing the multitudes, He [Jesus] felt compassion for them, because they were distressed and downcast like sheep without a shepherd.

²¹MARK 6

34 And when He went ashore, He saw a great multitude, and He felt compassion for them because they were like sheep without a shepherd; and He began to teach them many things.

²²JAMES 1

5-6 If any of you lacks wisdom, let him ask of God, who gives to all men generously and without reproach, and it will be given to him. But let him ask in faith without any doubting.

According to many scriptural passages, when left to our own limited reasoning we compare well to sheep. Read Jeremiah 50:6,[19] Matthew 9:36,[20] and Mark 6:34.[21] List some human attributes and conditions that relate to sheep.[T13]

Without God, we are like sheep without a shepherd. The areas of life where we need the insight and intervention of a divine Shepherd include applying Scripture and living our convictions, resolving conflict, developing relationships (assessing the character of others and understanding their needs), handling business and financial matters . . . the list is endless! With God's perspective, however, we can think through our circumstances and evaluate the possible outcomes in advance. Then we can avoid being caught off guard and discern how to respond rightly *before* we face any of life's inevitable issues. Divine insight and God's perspective are significant benefits of belonging to Him.

BRINGING IT HOME . . .

1. Do you ever feel like a "dumb sheep" or a "helpless lamb"—downcast? lost? even destroyed? Do you have a real need for wisdom and direction from the Good Shepherd? List the top two or three problems in your life (or in the life of your family or church) that are beyond your ability to resolve.

2. Read James 1:5-6,[22] then ask God for His divine insight and intervention into those circumstances you've listed above.

HISTORY & CULTURE:[T13]

ON SHEEP—Sheep are not known for their high intellect. They are totally dependent on a shepherd for their survival. Sheep make a good metaphor for us in our dependent relationship to God and in God's relationship to us as the Good Shepherd. For wonderful insights using analogies of people and sheep, read *A Shepherd's Look at Psalm 23* by Phillip Keller (Grand Rapids, MI: Zondervan, 1979).

DAILY READING

Read Proverbs 2:1-9. Mark the proverb that stands out most to you today.

[23] 1 CHRONICLES 21

16 Then David . . . saw the angel of the LORD standing between earth and heaven. . . . David and the elders . . . fell on their faces.

[24] DANIEL 8

1,16-17 In the third year of the reign of Belshazzar the king a vision appeared to me, Daniel. . . . And he called out and said, "Gabriel, give this man an understanding of the vision." So he came near . . . and when he came I was frightened and fell on my face.

[25] LUKE 5

4,6-9 He [Jesus] said to Simon, "Put out into the deep water and let down your nets." . . . They enclosed a great quantity of fish; and their nets began to break . . . and both of the boats . . . began to sink. But when Simon Peter saw that, he fell down at Jesus' feet, saying, "Depart from me, for I am a sinful man, O Lord!" For amazement had seized him.

[26] REVELATION 1

9-10,13,16-17 I, John . . . was in the Spirit . . . and . . . [I saw] one like a son of man . . . and His face was like the sun shining in its strength. And when I saw Him, I fell at His feet as a dead man.

Proverbs 1:7 is a key verse that not only tells us the source of wisdom but also establishes a pattern of contrasting the actions of the wise and the actions of the foolish—a contrast that runs throughout the entire book of Proverbs. According to Proverbs 1:7, what is the starting point for attaining wisdom?

When you hear the phrase "fear of God," what images come to mind?

What does it mean to fear the Lord? Isn't He a God of love? Yes! And He is also a God of wrath. He's a God of mercy and grace and a God of justice. The Lord describes Himself to Moses in Exodus 34:6-7:

"The LORD, the LORD God, compassionate and gracious, slow to anger, and abounding in lovingkindness and truth; who keeps lovingkindness for thousands, who forgives iniquity, transgression and sin; yet He will by no means leave the guilty unpunished."

God is not "either/or," God is "both/and." If only the body of Christ would accept the fullness of His character! Instead, we tend to create a distorted idea of God that is skewed, in one direction or the other, by our own ideologies. In an attempt to fit "the fear of God" into our Western concept of love, many believe (and teach) that fearing God simply means to honor and revere Him. And in fact, reverence is a component of fearing God. But there's more. For insight and understanding, we must let Scripture speak to Scripture (this is the essence of inductive study). Read 1 Chronicles 21:16;[23] Daniel 8:1,16-17;[24] Luke 5:4,6-9;[25] and excerpts of selected verses from Revelation 1.[26] (Note: The ellipses indicate that only the essence of the immediate context is provided. You may wish to read these verses in full in your

Bible.) Write the reaction of David, Daniel, Peter, and John to the physical manifestations of God's glory.

- David

- Daniel

- Peter

- John

The heroes of the faith responded to the manifestation of God with a knee-jerk reaction of sheer terror. We're told in the larger context of these Scriptures that these spiritual giants required supernatural strength through divine intervention just to stand before the angel of the Lord.[T14]

Another way we can gain insight into the seeming paradox of fearing a loving God is by looking up the Hebrew/Aramaic word for fear used in Proverbs 1:7 and comparing its meaning to other Hebrew words translated "fear." How are these words used in other Scripture passages? How are they alike? How do they differ?

There are more than ten Hebrew words that could be translated "fear." Each has a slightly different meaning in Hebrew. The Hebrew word most often used as "fear of the Lord," however, is *yirah* from the root word *yare*. *Yare* has a range of meanings; namely, "to be afraid, to fear, to revere" as well as "to be dreadful, to terrify." *Yirah* is defined by the same range of meanings as its root word, *yare*; but *yirah* alone includes the concept of "piety, religion, and worship."

Reverence and awe? Yes! And abject terror. The fear of the Lord is the heart-stopping realization of the glory, majesty, and power of God and of His right to absolute sovereignty over His creation. Without this realization, none of us will ever fall on our face before the Almighty. Worship happens when we are stricken in wonder that One so holy would invite us to live in relationship to Him—would have us call Him "Abba" Father.[T15] If we would be wise, we must begin by fearing God rightly.

HISTORY & CULTURE:[T14]
HUMAN ENCOUNTERS WITH GOD—God physically revealed Himself to people in a number of Old Testament encounters. Many of these encounters involved the angel of the Lord who (if He accepted worship) was, in fact, the "preincarnate Christ" (that is, God the Son before He became flesh in the person of Jesus). These appearances are called "theophanies." Read about some of these accounts.

For further study:
Genesis 18
Judges 6,13

POINT OF INTEREST:[T15]
GOD'S CHARACTER —
The different Hebrew names for God represent different aspects of His character. *Yahweh* is the most personal and most important name for God, for it shows God as a covenant keeper. It is this covenant-making, covenant-keeping part of God's character that is absolutely unique among all the religions of the world. *Yahweh* is ethical. *Yahweh* can be trusted. *Yahweh* is intimate and personal and, at the same time, awesome and transcendent (beyond our comprehension). When we get a glimpse of who *Yahweh* is—Creator, God Almighty, Sovereign Lord— our response will be fear, reverence, obedience, and worship.

For further study:
Malachi 3:17–4:3

²⁷ PSALMS

25:12-14 Who is the man who fears the LORD? He will instruct him. . . . His soul will abide in prosperity, and his descendants will inherit the land. The secret of the LORD is for those who fear Him, and He will make them know His covenant.

34:7,9 The angel of the LORD encamps around those who fear Him. . . . For to those who fear Him, there is no want.

103:13,17 Just as a father has compassion on his children, so the LORD has compassion on those who fear Him. . . . But the lovingkindness of the LORD is from everlasting to everlasting on those who fear Him, and His righteousness to children's children.

147:11 The LORD favors those who fear Him.

In addition to knowledge, there are tremendous benefits associated with fearing the Lord. Many are listed in Psalms and Proverbs.

Read the passages in Psalms[27] and look up the Proverbs in appendix A. Write down the benefits of fearing the Lord.

Psalm 25:12-14

34:7,9

103:13

103:17

147:11

Proverbs 10:27

14:26

16:6

22:4

THE BEGINNING OF KNOWLEDGE

Note that according to Proverbs 1:7, "The fear of the LORD is the beginning of knowledge." The Hebrew word for "beginning" is *reshith*, from the root word *rosh*, which means "head, topmost, summit." *Reshith* is the word used in Genesis 1:1, "In the beginning God. . . ." *Reshith* speaks of "hierarchy; the first in a sequence; headwaters." Notice *reshith* and *rosh* evoke images of origin and heights. We must not think of the fear of the Lord as a religious foundation upon which knowledge is built. *The fear of the Lord is, rather, like a conduit through which divine knowledge flows from the very fountainhead of truth.*

BRINGING IT HOME . . .

1. If possible, go outside (away from city lights), lie flat, and look at the heavens. As you gaze at the stars, consider that you're looking down as well as up and that the earth is but a tiny island of cosmic dust floating in infinite space. Against the vastness of space, how do you feel about your own importance? About the God who created all that you can see, feel, touch, smell, or perceive?

2. Spend a few minutes in personal worship, acknowledging God for who He is. Choose a favorite psalm or other passage about God's person and character. Praise Him for each attribute listed in that passage. Or meditate on the variety and intricacy of the created world and praise God for each attribute that creation reveals about Him.

3. Write Psalm 8:3-9 and Jeremiah 31:35-37 on a card or piece of paper and put it in your Bible to read tonight. Meditate on the wonder of being the most valued of all His creation.

DAILY READING
Read Proverbs 2:10-22. Mark the proverb that stands out most to you today.

DAY 3

KNOWING TRUTH

²⁸2 TIMOTHY 3

1-5 But realize this, that in the last days difficult times will come. For men will be lovers of self, lovers of money, boastful, arrogant, revilers, disobedient to parents, ungrateful, unholy, unloving, irreconcilable, malicious gossips, without self-control, brutal, haters of good, treacherous, reckless, conceited, lovers of pleasure rather than lovers of God; holding to a form of godliness, although they have denied its power; and avoid such men as these.

²⁹2 TIMOTHY 3

6-7 For among them are those [false teachers] who enter into households and captivate weak women weighed down with sins, led on by various impulses, always learning *[manthano]* and never able to come to the knowledge *[epignosis]* of the truth.

8-9 And just as Jannes and Jambres opposed Moses, so these men also oppose the truth, men of depraved mind, rejected [reprobate] as regards the faith . . . their folly will be obvious to all.

Have you ever known anyone who had a mind like a computer but who seemed unable to apply his or her own store of information in any practical way? People can have an incredible capacity to collect and retain "data" but, at the same time, be remarkably dysfunctional in their ability to make sense of it.

All knowledge is built on information (sensory as well as factual), but information does not necessarily lead to the knowledge of truth. Information must be rightly categorized, analyzed, and synthesized (blended together) to transform "info-bytes" into insight. As information is to knowledge, so knowledge is to wisdom. Knowledge is not wisdom, but it is the raw material that is cultivated into wisdom under submission to the Word of God and through the work of the Holy Spirit. *Wisdom is the outworking of the knowledge of truth.*

For most people, an information base is not hard to attain. But that which is worth knowing, that which is valuable, and that which is true begin with a singular heart condition, according to Proverbs 1:7. Write this beginning requirement again. It's too important to miss.

Because Scripture is absolute truth, isn't it an automatic source of knowledge, regardless of one's heart attitude? Can one read Scripture and conclude error? Think about this question a moment in light of Proverbs 1:7. Write down your thoughts.

Let's evaluate the idea of attaining knowledge about God through Scripture but without the fear of the Lord, without genuine recognition of the awesome power and sovereignty of God, and without acknowledging the authority of Scripture over our lives.

Read 2 Timothy 3:1-5.[28] Paul tells Timothy (and us) about false teachers who held to a form of godliness while denying the power of God. These men were not teaching an unrelated philosophy nor a different religion. They were salting the gospel with false information.

Do you think these teachers had been exposed to the truth? From what source were they attempting to teach?

Read about some students of these false teachers in 2 Timothy 3:6-7.[29]

What was the spiritual condition of these students?

▪

▪

How were they guided or led?

What were they always doing?

What always eluded them?

The Greek word used for "learning" in 2 Timothy 3:7 is *manthano*, which means "being educated, finding things out, receiving instruction." The women were absorbing the facts as presented, but did you catch what eludes them? Isn't that surprising? Don't we expect that anyone can gain the right *knowledge* (at least) from studying the Word of God, even if they don't attain great wisdom?

Let's look at this Scripture further. The Greek word used for "knowledge" (of the truth) in 2 Timothy 3:7 is *epignosis*. It means "to know exactly; to recognize and perceive." This knowledge has to do with more than just taking in correct data. It has to do with understanding, with making the right conclusions from the available information in order to arrive at truth.[T16]

Compare *epignosis* with the Hebrew word for "knowledge" (*daath*) from our key verse. *Daath*, "that which is known," is often translated as "truth." This word comes from the root word *yada*, which is translated in other Hebrew texts as "to become acquainted, to consider, to experience, to investigate, to observe, to take notice, to recognize, to perceive, to discern, and to

POINT OF INTEREST:[T16]
RIGHT DATA, WRONG ANSWERS—You know how funny children can be when they're learning to talk? You point to the family pet and say, "dog." Finally, your little one understands the name of this furry, four-legged creature. Next thing you know, he's showing off to the neighbors by proudly pointing to their pet and saying, "dog!" Cute. Except that the neighbor's dog is a cat. Why does the child call the cat a dog? Because his information base is too limited to judge rightly. His limited facts are correct—here *is* a furry, four-legged creature—but his knowledge is incomplete. Right data, wrong conclusion.

We may be a walking info-bank, even of Scripture, but we will always lack two things necessary to judge rightly: (1) complete, all-encompassing information and (2) the ability to discern truth through human reasoning. Human information, at best, is too full of holes. God Himself has to fill in the blanks.

For further study:
How does our intellect stack up to God's?

³⁰2 TIMOTHY 2

24-26 And the Lord's bond-servant must not be quarrel-some, but be kind to all, able to teach, patient when wronged, with gentleness correcting those who are in opposition, if perhaps God may grant them repentance leading to the knowledge of the truth, and they may come to their senses and escape from the snare of the devil.

³¹ 1 CORINTHIANS 2

14-16 But a natural man does not accept the things of the Spirit of God; for they are foolishness to him, and he cannot understand them, because they are spiritually appraised. But he who is spiritual appraises all things, yet he himself is appraised by no man. For who has known the mind of the Lord, that he should instruct Him? But we have the mind of Christ.

understand." Do you see the similarity between the meaning of the Hebrew word *daath* in Proverbs 1:7 ("the beginning of *knowledge*") and the meaning of the Greek word *epignosis* in 2 Timothy 3:7 ("the *knowledge* of truth")?

Let's examine another correlation. In our key verse (Proverbs 1:7), what precedes knowledge?

What precedes knowledge (of truth) according to 2 Timothy 2:24-26?[30]

Think about these two related Scriptures (Proverbs 1:7 and 2 Timothy 2:24-26). Do you see a common denominator? Read Proverbs 1:28-33. Write down your insights.

Let's look at one more New Testament Scripture as we conclude this day's study. Read 1 Corinthians 2:14-16.[31] What do Christians have that gives them access to the knowledge of truth?

How off-track we can get when we attempt to gain knowledge and wisdom apart from a right relationship with the Source of truth and wisdom. If we would know truth, we must begin by accepting our own ignorance and impotence apart from God and coming to Him with an attitude of reverential fear and repentance. Those who do will receive the mind of Christ, which will draw them into His Word with a heart bent toward obedience.[T17]

BRINGING IT HOME . . .

1. Think for a moment about a very close friend or your spouse. What was your first impression of this person? Was it positive? Negative? How has it changed as you have gotten to know the real person? Throughout this study your knowledge of God should be growing. In what ways is your response to His Word changing?

2. Are there any areas in your life where you might be more obedient if you had a fuller realization of God's sovereignty and power? Write down those things that come to mind, including specific ways they would change in the realized presence of God. Ask God to enable you to submit to His Word in these areas.

POINT OF INTEREST:[T17]

KNOWLEDGE OF TRUTH—History has proven over and over that people are capable of believing *anything*. It's remarkable how people can be incensed at the foolishness of past generations and the cruelty of other nations (such as Hitler's Germany) and be oblivious to similarities in their own behavior. Like those before us, we are an easily deluded people living in the midst of a wicked and perverse generation—in a world whose "prince" is the father of lies. Truth is elusive; who can know it?

Our lives are absolutely dictated by what we believe to be true. All that we do is meaningless if our life is based on a lie. In 2 Timothy 2:24-26,[30] we learn that repentance leads to the knowledge of the truth. In 1 Corinthians 2:14-16,[31] we learn that the things of God are spiritually appraised; on our own we cannot recognize truth when we see it. In John 14:6, Jesus said, "I am . . . the truth." How ironic that Truth was standing before Pilate all along—and Pilate missed Him.

Our Lord promised in John 8:31-32, "If you abide in My word, then you are truly disciples of Mine; and you shall know the truth, and the truth shall make you free." The words for discipline, diligence, knowledge, truth, wisdom, and freedom are repeatedly intertwined in Scripture after Scripture. If you have the Spirit of Truth in your life, then Truth Himself will be standing before your spiritual eyes as you study His Words. Whatever else you do, don't miss Him.

DAILY READING

Read Proverbs 3:1-12. Mark the proverb that stands out most to you today.

DAY 4

RECOGNIZING FOOLS

32 PROVERBS

1:22 How long, O naive [pathim] ones, will you love simplicity? And scoffers [litsim] delight themselves in scoffing, and fools [kesilim] hate knowledge?

8:5 O naive ones, discern prudence; And, O fools, discern wisdom.

9:6 Forsake your folly and live, and proceed in the way of understanding.

10:8 The wise of heart will receive commands, but a babbling fool [evilim] will be thrown down.

33 PSALMS

19:7 The testimony of the LORD is sure, making wise the simple.

116:6 The LORD preserves the simple.

119:130 The unfolding of Thy words gives light; It gives understanding to the simple.

We are born as raw material—valuable and precious in God's sight, but needing to be ordered so that our lives have meaning. Through discipline, we bring the chaotic, unstructured, raw material of our lives under the guidance of God's Word. We can do this because we've come to understand that His ways are higher than our ways and His thoughts are higher than our thoughts (Isaiah 55:9). We've recognized His sovereignty and His right to rule over His creation. And although we can't comprehend His glory, we understand that He is Lord God Almighty. We approach Him with reverential awe. We bow in worship and invite Him to refine us as silver and to shape and order our lives into something beautiful, something that pleases Him.[T18]

But what if we don't do these things? Then according to God's Word, we are a foolish people. Just *how* foolish we are depends upon the degree to which we are resisting the fear of the Lord. Do you remember (from unit 1, day 3) the Hebrew words for "receive" (*laqach:* "to capture, to seize") and for "instruction" (*musar:* "admonishment, correction, reproof, chastisement")? If we don't rightly fear God, we won't respect His authority over our lives. If we don't respect His authority, we will never willingly "receive" (seize) "instruction" (chastisement). In fact, we will come to despise instruction because the harder we resist the call of wisdom the deeper rebellion will become embedded in our spirits.

Proverbs uses four different Hebrew words for fool:

- *pathim:* naive or simple

- *kesilim:* dull or lacking sense

- *evilim:* actively opposing wisdom

- *litsim:* scoffers or scorners

The different types of fools are identified throughout Proverbs.[32] Through the use of these words, Proverbs shows the progressive intensity of foolish thinking and behaving as expressed by those who keep rejecting the call of wisdom. The meanings of these four words are expanded in the rest of today's study.

Pathim in the Hebrew is translated "the naive or the simple." It comes from the root word *pathah*, which means "spacious or wide open." *Pathim* describes most of us in our youth—aimless, uncommitted, no established convictions, open to suggestion, followers of the crowd. The naive are mentioned in Proverbs 1:22, 8:5, and 9:6.[32] Read these verses.

What does Wisdom ask the naive in Proverbs 1:22?

What do Proverbs 8:5 and 9:6 tell them (*pathim*) to do?

Read Psalms 19:7, 116:6, and 119:130.[33] Who preserves the naive according to these psalms?

What illuminates them?

Kesilim represent a worsening category of fools. *Kesilim* means "stupid or dull; ones lacking sense." *Kesilim* are not intellectually dull, but they are dull spiritually, insensitive to wisdom, thick, and antagonistic. Most of the "fools" in Proverbs are *kesilim*. They are found in Proverbs 3:35; 12:23; 13:19; 14:8,16; 15:20; 17:25; and 18:2,6 (among others). Read three (or more) of these Scriptures from appendix A.

How does Proverbs describe the *kesilim*?

Take heed! Some are worse than kesilim. Read Proverbs 26:12, 28:26, and 29:20. Who are they?

Evilim occupy the third level of descent in Proverb's gallery of fools. *Evilim* are the fools mentioned in our key verse (Proverbs 1:7). They despise wisdom and instruction, and love folly. They're not just antagonistic like the *kesilim*. The *evilim* actively oppose spiritual matters and

POINT OF INTEREST:[T18]
GOD'S INFINITE EXPERTISE—
There is no part of life where God's guidance is unrelated. We are prone to think, *God might know how to run a universe, but He can't figure out a profit and loss statement.* We think we know what's best in our own areas of expertise.

When the disciples had been out fishing all night, Jesus told them to cast their nets on the other side of the boat. Jesus was meddling in their area of expertise. Peter's response was a little cynical: "Lord, we've fished all night. . . . Nevertheless, at your will. . . ."

Can't you hear Peter mumbling under his breath, "What does He know? He knows for nothin' about fishing." The disciples failed to recognize the Lord's sovereignty until they caught so many fish they almost sunk the boat! God's abundant provision revealed the disciples' own inadequacy—right where they thought they were experts.

Are you trusting in your own "inadequacy" or are you inviting God to take the lead in your business, your occupation, your education, your finances, your family situations, and your life decisions? If you're not trusting God, you're losing the expertise of the most knowledgeable mentor you could ever hope to have. Stop now and ask Him to begin teaching you to lean on His all sufficiency.

For further study:
What part does God play in your plans?
(Proverbs 16:7)
What are God's plans for you?
(Jeremiah 29:11)

[34]PSALM 1

1-2 How blessed is the man who does not walk in the counsel of the wicked, nor stand in the path of sinners, nor sit in the seat of scoffers! But his delight is in the law of the LORD, and in His law he meditates day and night.

hold wisdom in disdain. Proverbs speaks of the *evilim* in 10:8,21; 14:9; 15:5; 20:3; 27:22; and 29:9 (among others). Read at least three of these verses and write Proverbs' descriptions of the foolish *evilim*.

Litsim (translated "scoffers or scorners") are on the bottom rung of the ladder of fools. These are cynics, people full of arrogance and pride who despise those submitted to the will and rule of God. The *litsim* are mentioned in Proverbs 3:33-34, 9:7-8, 13:1, 19:28-29, 21:24, 22:10, and 24:9. Write what you learn from reading several of these verses.

Psalm 1:1-2[34] gives us a picture of a scoffer (or scorner). According to these verses, how do "the blessed" interact with scoffers? How do you interact with them?

BRINGING IT HOME . . .

1. At times we all can and will be foolish. With which category of fools do you identify? From the things you've learned so far, what are some keys to staying free from folly?

2. Not being teachable is an obvious hindrance to receiving wisdom. Do you have any "pet" beliefs that you are unwilling to hold up against God's Word for fear you might be wrong? Are there subjects you avoid studying seriously because the outcome might demand a change in the way you live? Write those subjects or beliefs down and confess them to God as areas of resistance. Pick one subject and begin taking a serious look at it from the whole counsel of God. Ask God to break any part of your theology or life philosophies that aren't in agreement with His Word.

DAILY READING
Read Proverbs 3:13-24. Mark the proverb that stands out most to you today.

DAY 5

DESPISING WISDOM AND INSTRUCTION

Our key verse, Proverbs 1:7, tells us that fools (specifically the *evilim*) despise wisdom and instruction. As we learned yesterday, the *evilim* are not just naive or even spiritually dull and insensitive. The *evilim* reject knowledge, hold wisdom in disdain, and actively oppose spiritual matters.[T19] Read of the *evilim* (fool) in Proverbs 10:21 (in appendix A) and Hosea 4:6.[35]

Why were the people destroyed?

Who rejected knowledge and forgot God's law?

Read the priests' responsibilities in regard to God's wisdom and instruction as recorded in Malachi 2:7-8:

> "For the lips of a priest should preserve knowledge, and men should seek instruction from his mouth; for he is the messenger of the LORD of hosts. But as for you, you have turned aside from the way; you have caused many to stumble by the instruction; you have corrupted the covenant of Levi," says the LORD of hosts.

The priests rejected God's words of wisdom. Based on both Hosea 4:6 and Malachi 2:7-8, what were the consequences?

Read Jeremiah 8:9.[36] Why are the wise men put to shame?

Rejection of God's Word by the leaders of Israel, both its kings and its priests, was an all-too-familiar story. Read the condition of Israel described in Isaiah 1:21-23.[37] Sounds a bit like our society today, doesn't it?

---

[35] HOSEA 4

6 "My people are destroyed for lack of knowledge. Because you have rejected knowledge, I also will reject you from being My priest. Since you have forgotten the law of your God, I also will forget your children."

[36] JEREMIAH 8

9 "The wise men are put to shame, they are dismayed and caught; Behold, they have rejected the word of the LORD, and what kind of wisdom do they have?"

[37] ISAIAH 1

21-23 "How the faithful city has become a harlot, she who was full of justice! Righteousness once lodged in her, but now murderers. Your silver has become dross, your drink diluted with water. Your rulers are rebels, and companions of thieves; Everyone loves a bribe, and chases after rewards. They do not defend the orphan, nor does the widow's plea come before them."

[38] ISAIAH 1

24-26 Therefore the Lord God of hosts, the Mighty One of Israel declares . . . "I will also turn My hand against you, and will smelt away your dross as with lye, and will remove all your alloy. Then I will restore your judges as at the first, and your counselors as at the beginning; After that you will be called the city of righteousness, a faithful city."

On day 4, we mentioned inviting God to refine us as silver. *Refining* means "to reduce to a pure state by removing imperfections." Silver, as an ore, is full of lead and other impurities called dross. Consider how silver is refined. It is fired (heated) in a crucible until the silver ore liquifies and releases its dross. A silversmith skims the impurities off the top, and then gradually increases the temperature until more and more of the dross is released. The heating-skimming process is repeated until the silversmith can see his reflection clearly on the surface of the molten metal.

When Scripture speaks of God's "refining His people as silver," it speaks of the fiery circumstances God may permit for the purpose of removing our moral imperfections, great and small. Read Isaiah 1:24-26[38] (also review Psalm 119:67,71[12]). When God refines (tries) us, what are the results?

Why do you think it sometimes takes painful circumstances to get us to the point that we "release the dross" in our lives?

Refining is for our good and Christlikeness. Remember when we talked about people being like sheep? If a lamb is prone to wander, the shepherd will break the lamb's leg and then carry it until the lamb's leg heals. This is the only way the shepherd can keep the foolish lamb from straying toward its certain death. Having "bonded" to the shepherd during its brokenness, the restored lamb will henceforth remain close to the shepherd.[T13] God's refining is sometimes painful, but it drives us toward the good Shepherd for healing. Christians who would reflect God's image must willingly submit to the refining process.

God also uses affliction to call sinners to Himself (Psalm 119:67,71[12]), but sometimes, people just won't respond. They are like silver ore that will not release its dross, no matter how hot the temperature gets!

POINT OF INTEREST:[T19]
ULTIMATE CONSEQUENCES OF REJECTING WISDOM—
The consequences of behaving wisely or foolishly may not be realized immediately but will be realized ultimately. In spite of all the absurdities of our culture with its great inequities and injustices, God will not be mocked. His holiness, sovereignty, and wrath are just as fundamental to His character as His compassion, mercy, and grace.

It is our responsibility to respond to God's call. Continual rejection of His call will cause us to develop such a calloused heart that God will eventually let us have our way, to our own destruction. A good example is Pharaoh of Egypt. God sent Moses again and again to tell Pharaoh to let Israel go. And again and again Pharaoh hardened his heart (Exodus 8:15,19,32 and 9:7,34). There came a point, however, when God Himself hardened Pharaoh's heart in order that He "may perform these signs of Mine among them, and that you may tell in the hearing of your son, and of your grandson, how I made a mockery of the Egyptians, and how I performed My signs among them; that you may know that I am the LORD" (Exodus 10:1-2).

If this world were all there would ever be, we would be a frustrated people because from our perspective many people seem to get away with outrageous actions. But God says, "No! I will use even your rebellion to gain glory for My name and gain souls for my kingdom." And at the end of the day, all will stand before God who will bring all things to light.

For further study:
Psalm 37:1-22
Titus 1:15-16

27-30 "I have made you an assayer [one who determines if there are any valuable components to metal ores] and a tester among My people, that you may know and assay their way." All of them are stubbornly rebellious, Going about as a talebearer.

They are bronze and iron; They, all of them, are corrupt. The bellows blow fiercely, the lead is consumed by the fire; In vain the refining goes on, but the wicked are not separated. They call them rejected [maas] silver, because the LORD has rejected them.

Read Jeremiah 6:27-30.[39]

What does God call those who stubbornly hold to their wickedness or perhaps to unbiblical religious beliefs?[T20]

Why does He call them that?

The Hebrew word for rejected is *maas*. *Maas* means "unaccepted, condemned as worthless; not standing the test; reprobate, evil." In the New Testament the Greek counterpart is *adokimos*, which means "not standing the test, depraved, disqualified, rejected, worthless, reprobate." First, read the use of *adokimos* meaning "rejected" in 2 Timothy 3:8-9,[29] and then read the abridged Romans 1:18-22,25-32 below (or better still, read the entire passage from your Bible):

> For the wrath of God is revealed from heaven against all ungodliness and unrighteousness of men, who suppress the truth, . . . because that which is known about God is evident within them; for God made it evident to them. . . . His invisible attributes, His eternal power and divine nature, have been clearly seen, being understood through what has been made, so that they are without excuse. For even though they knew God, they did not honor Him as God, or give thanks; but they became futile in their speculations, and their foolish heart was darkened. Professing to be wise, they became fools. . . . For they exchanged the truth of God for a lie. . . . For this reason God gave them over to degrading passions. . . . And just as they did not . . . acknowledge God, . . . God gave them over to a depraved [reprobate (*adokimos*)] mind . . . being filled with all unrighteousness, . . . haters of God, insolent, arrogant, boastful, inventors of evil, disobedient to parents, without understanding, untrustworthy, unloving, unmerciful; and, although they know the ordinance of God, that those who practice such things are worthy of death, they not only do the same, but also give hearty approval to those who practice them.

A reprobate is one who continually rejects the Word of God, the truth of God, the Spirit of God, and the grace of God until he or she ultimately faces the wrath of God. In His love and mercy, however, God is offering salvation, even to the scoffer—the fool in full rebellion. We must not refuse Him, for "who can endure the day of His coming? And who can stand when He appears? For He is like a refiner's fire. . . . And He will sit as a smelter and purifier of silver, and he will purify the sons of Levi . . ." (Malachi 3:2-3).

BRINGING IT HOME . . .

1. Part of the refining process is allowing God to remove the "dross" in our lives. Think of all areas of your life: relational, moral, spiritual, intellectual. Write down any recurring problem areas or trigger points in your life. Is it possible that God is refining you? Bring these things before the Lord asking Him to refine you as He sees fit.

2. Do you have a family member or friend who is resisting God's love and discipline? Make a commitment to pray for this person daily and begin today!

POINT OF INTEREST:[T20]

THE TRAP OF RELIGIOSITY— The problem with religion is that it can encourage a pseudo-salvation—an external change of life apart from an internal change of heart. It's quite easy, actually, to generally do right things, say right things, go to church services—whatever. You may enjoy a community of worshipers, but beyond that, "religion" won't do you any good. God has to do something to your heart, something internal, before you can become a part of His kingdom. And God has to do something to your heart before you'll ever understand that His truths are far deeper than rules of doctrine and rituals of worship.

For further study:
Are you His?
How about your heart?
(Ezekiel 33:29-33; 11:19-20)
(John 3:3-8)
(Ephesians 1:15-18)
(See also "God's Plan of Salvation," appendix B.)

DAILY READING

Read Proverbs 3:25-33 and mark the proverb that stands out most to you today. Review all the proverbs you marked this week and select one to memorize.

To the leader: For this time together have the blank chart from question 4 displayed.

1. All of us have been influenced by the counsel and insights of others. Take a few moments to reflect on the wisest person you know personally.
   - What are the qualities that make this person so wise? As a group list all the characteristics as they are mentioned.
   - As a group, read aloud Proverbs 3:1-26. Add any additional traits of a wise person to your list.

2. Share with the group how you best approach God:
   —With fear and reverence
   —With the boldness and spontaneity of a child saying, "Daddy"
   - Why do you think this is true?
   - How might these two seemingly paradoxical concepts be reconciled?

3. Decide whether you agree or disagree with this statement: "It is possible to be always learning and never come to the knowledge of truth."
   - Why or why not? Support your answer with Scriptures from unit 2 (pages 29-50).
   - Share a new truth you have discovered as a result of this study and how you are applying it in your life.
   - Name some widely held false doctrines within our culture today. In what ways are they based on either misreading of Scripture or taking verses out of context?

4. The book of Proverbs teaches about four types of fools. Divide into four groups (a "group" can be one person) and have each group review one of the four types of fools listed. After about five minutes reconvene and have one person from each group complete the appropriate portion of the following chart (which has been written on a board or flipchart).

Hebrew	Translated as	Characteristics	Result of their behavior
Pethim			
Kesilim			
Evilim			
Litsim			

5. English author C. S. Lewis said that pain—whether physical or emotional—is God's megaphone to get our attention. Share examples of how God has used pain in your own life and the lives of other believers (who you know personally or who are public figures) and the results.
   - How does God use pain (or refining) in the lives of believers?
   - A reprobate is one who continually rejects the Word of God, the truth of God, the Spirit of God, and the grace of God. In other words, the one who ultimately rejects Jesus. Read Psalm 37:1-22. What will happen to those who continually turn from God?

Get in pairs to close in prayer. With your partner, share the truth you mentioned in question 3. Pray for each other and for the wisdom and power to apply the truth on a consistent basis throughout the week.

INTRODUCTION TO UNIT 3
UNDERSTANDING DIVINE WISDOM

Destination: To develop a biblical understanding of divine wisdom—how it is different from human wisdom and how it relates to salvation.

As a consulting science writer, I (Gail) have often served on engineering projects involving several companies. On one such project I met a scientist, originally from India, who told me he was a Christian. "Oh!" I said. "I had assumed you were Hindu."

"I am Hindu," the man explained. "But now that I'm a citizen of a Christian nation, I'm a Christian Hindu." His conclusion jammed my cognitive circuits. Trying to comprehend such a theological hybrid was like trying to picture a round square. I was speechless.

One of my Bible students shared that she had a similar surprise when she encouraged a woman in her fifties to read the book of John. "John?" the woman replied, "What's that?" Such a fundamental ignorance of the Bible is difficult to comprehend—at least by those who have been nurtured on biblical teaching.

The general knowledge of God and His ways have essentially vanished from our culture; and that change is disturbing. More disturbing, however, is that sound Christian theology is only superficially understood by many, if not most, of the people who are active in churches today—including evangelical churches. The description from Hebrews 5:11-14 may be too accurate:

> We have much to say, and *it is* hard to explain, since you have become dull of hearing. For though by this time you ought to be teachers, you have need again for someone to teach you the elementary principles of the oracles of God, and you have come to need milk and not solid food. For everyone who partakes *only* of milk is not accustomed to the word of righteousness, for he is a babe. But solid food is for the mature. . . .

Many congregations receive limited exposure to the Bible, much less to any systematic study of Scripture. But even those who grew up in Bible-teaching churches may have only a child's understanding of the gospel. This is not "childlike faith" but a failure to mature in the Word. Often we don't even recognize our limited knowledge because we've absorbed a religious vocabulary and we can (and do) freely use Christian jargon, even in the right context. The moment of truth comes, however, when someone asks us to explain a salvation concept, like "redemption" or "justification," and we draw a mental blank.

In unit 3, we will seek to gain a more in-depth understanding of wisdom, especially as it relates to salvation. Deeper understanding of any subject requires diligent study, and study takes time. But the rewards are great as we apply wisdom to service within the body of Christ, "until we all attain to the unity of the faith, and of the knowledge of the Son of God, to a mature man, to the measure of the stature which belongs to the fullness of Christ" (Ephesians 4:13). As we begin this unit, pray that God will give you insight and a mature understanding of divine wisdom.

DAY 1

HUMAN WISDOM AND DIVINE WISDOM

⁴⁰JAMES 3

13-17 Who among you is wise and understanding? Let him show by his good behavior his deeds in the gentleness of wisdom. But if you have bitter jealousy and selfish ambition in your heart, do not be arrogant and so lie against the truth. This wisdom is not that which comes down from above, but is earthly, natural, demonic. For where jealousy and selfish ambition exist, there is disorder and every evil thing. . . . Wisdom from above is first pure, then peaceable, gentle, reasonable, full of mercy and good fruits, unwavering, without hypocrisy.

⁴¹GALATIANS 5

22-23 The fruit of the Spirit is love, joy, peace, patience, kindness, goodness, faithfulness, gentleness, self-control.

⁴²JOHN 8

44 "You are of your father the devil, and you want to do the desires of your father. He was a murderer from the beginning, and does not stand in the truth, because there is no truth in him. Whenever he speaks a lie, he speaks from his own nature; for he is a liar, and the father of lies."

As we've studied in the previous chapters, "wisdom" in the Hebrew language includes the idea of gaining a skill. The skills associated with the wisdom of Proverbs relate to morality, practical righteousness, and integrity. This wisdom, divine in origin, has a spiritual component that gives its possessors uncommon insight and understanding; it allows them to react with discipline, discernment, and discretion.

Because the source is God Himself, true wisdom is an expression of God's character, His attributes, and His perfection; that is, His righteousness, justice, faithfulness, holiness, moral purity, ethical goodness, and love. Obviously, then, the divine wisdom of Proverbs differs from wisdom attained by human aspirations. God-centered wisdom, a gift by grace, is fathomless. Human-centered wisdom, an attempt at success by works, is bound by the limits of our own humanity.[T21]

Both the Old Testament and the New Testament tell us that earthly, human-centered wisdom can attain for us some measure of worldly success; however, earthly wisdom will take us only so far, eventually lead us off track, and never help us attain unto God. A wonderful contrast of earthly and divine wisdom is found in James 3:13-17.[40] James twice mentions the same two pride-based characteristics that reveal human-centered wisdom. What are they?

-
-

James says the wisdom that "is not that which comes down from above" is:

-
-
-

Worldly wisdom involves the "natural" motivators for worldly success; namely, to get even (bitter jealousy) and to get ahead of others (selfish ambition). By its very "sin" nature, James says, human-centered wisdom is earthly, natural, and demonic. Earthly wisdom is not from earth at

all—it's from hell. The wisdom of the world comes from the prince of this world, who uses jealousy to incite us to manipulate others for our own personal gain and hoarding. His goal, however, is to fulfill his own purpose and desire; namely, our destruction. Not so with divine wisdom! Read James 3:13-17[40] again. List the words James uses to describe divine wisdom (or "wisdom from above").

- ▪   ▪
- ▪   ▪
- ▪   ▪
- ▪   ▪

Read Galatians 5:22-23.[41] What similarities do you see between the Galatians list and the characteristics of "wisdom from above" according to James?

What does Paul say is the *source* of the characteristics listed in Galatians 5:22-23?

By now, this isn't news. We've already discovered in unit 1 that truth comes from God. Even when it comes through human pathways, such as pastors, parents, or elders, and even when it deals with mundane observations of human life, uncorrupted truth is from God.

Earthly wisdom is demonic, but is it untrue? Read John 8:44.[42] Satan is called the father of what?

What is absent in Satan's nature?

If God is the Source of truth and Satan has *no truth* in him, then why are we so easily deceived? Why are we prone to embrace earthly wisdom above divine wisdom? Perhaps it's because earthly, human-centered wisdom is so appealing to our human desires or lusts—our appetites, greed, and pride.

POINT OF INTEREST:[T21]

RESISTING OUR BEST GOOD— If God would come to us on our own terms, we would endure only the amount of transformation necessary to have our way. Suppose that God's plan allowed simple acknowledgment and belief in Christ. And suppose that once we agreed, the Lord's power would be ours upon demand; that is, all our prayers would be answered immediately, exactly as we prayed! What do you think life would be like? What do you think we would be like? Arrogant perhaps? Complacent?

Certainly we would be stymied in our growth and maturity because no one ever really grows morally or spiritually from ease and success. Courage, character, patience, and fortitude—qualities we admire in others—are forged in pain, failures, and hardship. If we could choose our own way, we would be destroyed, because we haven't a clue as to what our "best good" looks like. Don't you, even now, thank God for some unanswered prayers?

For further study:
James 4:3

⁴³ 1 JOHN 2

16 For all that is in the world, the lust of the flesh and the lust of the eyes and the boastful pride of life, is not from the Father, but is from the world.

⁴⁴ ROMANS 8

16-18 The Spirit Himself bears witness with our spirit that we are children of God, and if children, heirs also . . . with Christ, if indeed we suffer with Him in order that we may also be glorified with Him. For . . . the sufferings of this present time are not worthy to be compared with the glory that is to be revealed to us.

Read 1 John 2:16.⁴³ What is the source of our lusts and our pride?

Earthly, worldly wisdom always centers on getting its own selfish desires met—on immediate gratification. Further, earthly wisdom always abandons the commandments of God and the lordship of Jesus, avoids thinking about the consequences (or even of getting caught), and asserts itself through self-indulgence, self-rule, and self-sufficiency. Earthly wisdom is delusion by the father of lies—a mastermind who traps us by our own sin nature and pride.

Yet while the enemy of our souls affirms our self-importance, Jesus says, "Let him who is the greatest among you become as the youngest, and the leader as the servant" (Luke 22:26). In Romans 12:16, Paul exhorted the church by saying, "Do not be haughty in mind, but associate with the lowly. Do not be wise in your own estimation."

We saw in James 3⁴⁰ that earthly wisdom is fraught with jealousy and selfish ambition. How does earthly wisdom compare to the attributes of a Christian in these verses from Luke and Romans?

Earthly wisdom feeds and fuels our bitter jealousies and selfish ambitions. Divine wisdom calls us to dependence, humility, and more. Read Romans 8:16-18.⁴⁴ What does divine wisdom call us to endure with Christ?

What God has in mind for us greatly exceeds anything we could ever imagine. Christlikeness and heaven will ultimately be realized only through suffering. Can you see the rub? In the immediate, where our flesh abides, divine wisdom has limited "curb appeal." ᵀ²² Thus we would never choose it for ourselves because our "selves" are enslaved to sin. Fallen humans cannot escape the gravitational pull of Satan's corrupted wisdom. That, my friend, takes the power of the Cross.

BRINGING IT HOME . . .

1. Consider your attitudes toward material possessions and work. Do you own things? Or do they own you? Do you work to live (eat)? Or do you live to work? Would you define your ambition as more often healthy or selfish? Decide on one thing you can change to move away from selfish ambition. Ask God for His enabling power and start the change today.

2. Review "Point of Interest:[T22] The Problem with Curb Appeal." Is there anything in your life right now that has great "curb appeal" but has let you down? Based on 1 John 2:16,[43] what enticed you? Now ask God what He wants you to do with this situation. Share His answer with a close friend who will keep you accountable in this area.

POINT OF INTEREST:[T22]

THE PROBLEM WITH CURB APPEAL—Imagine two houses, each flanked on both sides by close-growing hedges and tall trees. The first is tidy but small, modest, and more costly. The second is disorderly, but has three stories and is quite grand. By common sense, you buy the grand house, imagining how impressed your friends will be. Then you step through the front door and . . . into your backyard. There is no home inside—there is no inside at all. The little bungalow, on the other hand, has bright new rooms that open up throughout one's lifetime, and its back door is a threshold to paradise.

The problem with common sense choices is that they're so *common*. Only *uncommon* sense would have chosen the neater home with less "curb appeal." In our flesh, we couldn't have known because human choices are based, at best, on incomplete information and limited insight.

It's always best to ask God for uncommon sense from an uncommon source—divine revelation by the Divine Revealer.

DAILY READING

Read Proverbs 4:1-13. Mark the proverb that stands out most to you today.

DAY 2

WISDOM AND HUMILITY

⁴⁵EZEKIEL 28

12-17,19 "Take up a lamentation over the king of Tyre, and say to him, 'thus says the Lord God, "You had the seal of perfection, full of wisdom. . . . You were in Eden. . . . You were the anointed cherub who covers, . . . blameless in your ways from the day you were created, until unrighteousness was found in you. By the abundance of your trade you were internally filled with violence, and you sinned; Therefore I have cast you as profane From the mountain of God. And I have destroyed you. . . . Your heart was lifted up because of your beauty; You corrupted your wisdom by reason of your splendor. I cast you to the ground. . . . And you will be no more."'"

⁴⁶ISAIAH 14

12-15 How you have fallen from heaven, O star of the morning, son of the dawn! You have been cut down to the earth . . . weakened the nations! But you said in your heart, "I will ascend to heaven; I will raise my throne above the stars of God, And I will sit on the mount of assembly In the recesses of the north. . . . I will make myself like the Most High." Nevertheless you will be thrust down to Sheol, To the recesses of the pit.

⁴⁷1 PETER 5

8 Your adversary, the devil, prowls about like a roaring lion, seeking someone to devour.

In yesterday's excursion, we learned that true wisdom is divine and that earthly, worldly wisdom is demonic. We also learned that earthly wisdom asserts itself in pride and autonomy (self-rule). Satan is referred to in Ezekiel as the "king of Tyre," as well as the "covering cherub," and in Isaiah as the "star of the morning." Read Ezekiel 28:12-17,19[45] and Isaiah 14:12-15.[46] Basically, what was Satan's intent?

Though created in perfection, Satan *corrupted* his own wisdom. Notice that Satan didn't abandon truth for full-blown lies. Instead, he tainted his wisdom with enough truth to be believable, enough allure to be desirable, and enough error to be damnable. In fact, tainting the truth worked so well in the Garden of Eden that Satan has never since changed his devices! It would be better for us if his attacks were blatant—if everything hostile to our physical and spiritual well-being were obvious and ugly. But life isn't that way. Satan tantalizes our appetites and our pride with illusions of good things in an arrogant attempt to destroy God's good purposes for our lives. (Read 1 Peter 5:8.[47])

Attempting to usurp God's throne is the ultimate act of pride. His attempt to dethrone the King of kings reduced Satan from the greatest of angels to the enemy of God. How did God respond to Satan's pride?

Contrast the arrogance of the "prince of this planet" and the humility of the Lord God Almighty! Creator! King of heaven and earth! In Matthew, Jesus said of Himself:

8:20: "The foxes have holes, and the birds of the air have nests; but the Son of Man has nowhere to lay His head."

11:29: "Take My yoke upon you, and learn from Me, for I am gentle and humble in heart; and you shall find rest for your souls."

20:28: "The Son of Man did not come to be served, but to serve, and to give His life a ransom for many."

What are the proud after? Knowledge? Power? Riches? Honor? *All* of these. In themselves these things are not wrong. They become a problem when we seek them for our own glory. How does God respond to our pride? How does He respond to our humility? Read the Proverbs below from appendix A. Note what you see.

PROVERBS	PROUD/ARROGANT	HUMBLE
8:13		
11:2		
16:5		
16:18		
29:23		

Also read the verses from Psalms 10, 25, and 37.[48] List some benefits of humility below.

That which prideful man greedily grasps (to his own destruction) is a mere by-product of humility. By the way, do these benefits of humility sound familiar? (If not, review unit 2, day 2.) Review the verses from Psalms 25, 34, 103, and 147[27] and Proverbs 15:33 and 22:4 in appendix A. What are some benefits of humility?

Like mirror images of one another, the "fear of the Lord" and "humility" both reflect the realization of who God is and who we are in relation to Him.[T23] The first shines a light on God; the second shines His light on us—a light that reveals our guilt, even our most deeply hidden sins. We cannot be exposed to His light and remain unchanged; for when our eyes are opened to our own depravity, we are undone. His light will either drive us to Him for salvation or drive us away in shame, rebellion, or denial. And if we are His, we *will* be convicted of sin.

POINT OF INTEREST:[T23]
CONVICTION OF SIN—
One thing that marks true believers is conviction of sin. When children of God knowingly violate the Father's commandments, they are convicted, sorry, and repentant.

If you can continue to disobey what you know are God's mandates without any sense of conviction, you should seriously question whether or not you have God's Spirit in you. Scripture indicates that if you lack conviction and repentance, you have no real basis for assurance of salvation. It's true that the objective basis of salvation is the blood of Christ. But the *sense* of assurance is based on obedience and responsiveness to God's Word and will. Absence of this assurance is not trivial! Be sure that Christ is really in your life!

For further study:
2 Corinthians 13:5
2 Peter 1:1-11
1 John 3:18-22

Denial of guilt, by the way, is not limited to the unchurched. In America today, many people claim to embrace some Christian-oriented belief system, but most have never acknowledged their own sinfulness. In fact, a number of once-orthodox Protestant denominations now embrace a theology of the "goodness of man," whereby one can attain unto God by good deeds. This worldly wisdom is the antithesis of Scripture from Genesis to Revelation! Consider these New Testament texts:

1 John 1:10: If we say that we have not sinned, we make Him [God] a liar, and His word is not in us.

Romans 5:12: Therefore, just as through one man [Adam] sin entered into the world, and death through sin, and so death spread to all men, because all sinned.

1 John 3:7-8: Little children let no one deceive you . . . the one who practices sin is of the devil; for the devil has sinned from the beginning.

Unfortunately it is easy to deny our own guilt. What do you think is the danger of this self-deception? Why is this attitude the most dangerous of all aspects of pride?

Denial of guilt before a holy God is the most dangerous of all acts of pride because it keeps us from confessing our sin and from calling upon God in humility and repentance. It is the height of folly, pride, and arrogance to suppose we can attain through our own efforts those things that only God provides, and has provided, by humbling Himself unto death, even death on a cross.[T24] The marvelous truth in Scripture is this: God intends for each of us to abandon our own efforts and to humbly receive His gift of eternal life, given by grace, received by faith in Jesus Christ, through the work of His Holy Spirit.

Read Isaiah 66:2.[49] Do you desire an audience with God? How should you then approach Him?

BRINGING IT HOME . . .

1. Ask yourself the following questions: Am I obedient to what God has already revealed to me in His Word? Are there any actions or desires in my life that I'm afraid to look at in light of His Word?

2. With your eyes closed, picture Jesus walking into your home. Ask yourself: Are there any books, magazines, videos, pictures, or other things I wouldn't want Him to see? Would I show Him my closets? Would I want Him to see the spending entries in my checkbook?

3. Knowing that a person's home usually reveals something about the extent of his or her relationships—mementos, family pictures, hobbies—ask yourself: Is there anything in my home that would make it obvious to Jesus that I love Him?

　　In prayer, be honest about your answers to these questions. Ask the Lord for the wisdom and strength to eliminate what is displeasing to Him and to add what is needed to bring you closer to Him.

POINT OF INTEREST:[T24]

A GOD WHO SEEKS US—
In Anuradhapura, Sri Lanka, there is the sacred Bo tree, which is supposedly derived from the original Bodhi-Tree under which the Buddha claimed to have attained enlightenment. Even now, in that ruined city, the Bo tree is worshiped by thousands. The Bo tree is to the Buddhist as the cross is to the Christian. This contrast is very instructive. The Bo tree symbolizes human attempts to reach up to God, whereas the cross, where Christ hung between heaven and earth, symbolizes God's reaching down to humanity. This difference is the perfect picture of our attempts to reach and attain life on our own terms versus God's reaching down and closing the gap between us and Him— something we cannot do for ourselves. This is the uniqueness of the Judeo-Christian vision; namely, a God who seeks us in contrast to our seeking Him on our own.

DAILY READING

Read Proverbs 4:14-27. Mark the proverb that stands out most to you today.

DAY 3

WISDOM AND REPENTANCE

[50] JOB 42

5-6 I have heard of Thee by the hearing of the ear; But now my eye sees Thee; Therefore I retract *[maas]*, and I repent *[nacham]* in dust and ashes.

[51] JEREMIAH 31

19 For after I turned back *[shub]*, I repented *[nacham]*; And after I was instructed, I smote on my thigh; I was ashamed, and also humiliated, because I bore the reproach of my youth.

[52] PSALM 34

18 The LORD is near to the brokenhearted, and saves those who are crushed in spirit.

[53] ISAIAH 6

6-8 Then one of the seraphim . . . with a burning coal . . . touched my mouth . . . and said, "Behold . . . your iniquity is taken away, and your sin is forgiven." Then I heard . . . the Lord, saying, "Whom shall I send, and who will go for Us?" Then I said, "Here am I. Send me!"

[54] JEREMIAH 6

26 O daughter of my people, put on sackcloth and roll in ashes; Mourn as for an only son, a lamentation most bitter.

[55] MATTHEW 11

21 "Woe to you, Bethsaida! For if the miracles had occurred in Tyre and Sidon which occurred in you, they would have repented *[metanoeo]* long ago in sackcloth and ashes."

God's truths abound—in Scripture, in godly teaching, even in creation. However, human reasoning cannot differentiate between "earthly wisdom" and "wisdom from above" because (as we've already seen) the knowledge of divine truth begins with the fear of the Lord and responds with humility. We've also seen that the forerunner of the knowledge of divine truth is *repentance* (2 Timothy 2:24-26[30]). "Repentance" is a term that is as richly used in Christian circles as it is poorly understood. Part of the problem lies in the limitations of language in translation. Another part is that we as Christians have failed to preserve the biblical integrity of the word and have allowed its meaning of salvation to degenerate. Therefore, in today's study we will look back to the biblical concept of repentance and to the relationship of repentance to wisdom.

REPENTANCE IN THE OLD TESTAMENT HEBREW

There are two distinctive but complementary concepts regarding the idea of repentance in Hebrew. The first is embodied in the word *nacham*. *Nacham* means "to be sorry, to regret, to appease." It is a time of mourning. The other concept is expressed in the related Hebrew words *shub* and *maas*. *Shub* means "to turn back, return, remake, restore, revive." *Maas* means "to completely reject, to abhor, to disdain, and to retract." Both of these concepts are explicit in the Hebrew understanding of repentance as it leads to salvation.

Read Job 42:5-6,[50] Jeremiah 31:19,[51] and Psalm 34:18.[52] What caused Job to turn and mourn?

What caused Jeremiah's shame and sorrow?

Although expressed differently, both Job's and Jeremiah's repentance reflect the common human reaction to seeing oneself by the light of God's holiness.

Job repented at the sight of God; Jeremiah, in the light of God. Job repented due to the fear of the Lord; Jeremiah repented out of humility. Remember the reactions of David, Daniel, Peter, and John when they encountered God's glory (unit 2, day 2)? When Isaiah saw the Lord, the King, and heard the seraphim shouting, "Holy, Holy, Holy, is the LORD of hosts" (Isaiah 6:3), he confessed, "Woe is me, for I am ruined! Because I am a man of unclean lips" (Isaiah 6:5).

Read Isaiah 6:6-8.[53] How was Isaiah changed as a result of this encounter?

Who changed Isaiah?

How did he then respond to God's call for someone to "go" for us?

REPENTANCE IN THE NEW TESTAMENT GREEK

The Greek word for "repent," *metanoeo*, means "to change one's mind and purpose." *Metanoeo* is a good example of a word translation that does not, by itself, explicitly carry the Hebrew concept of mourning—at least not with the same weight as it does the concept of changing and turning around. Nevertheless, both mourning and turning are clearly implied in the New Testament as well. Compare Old Testament verses in Job 42:5-6[50] and Jeremiah 6:26[54] with Matthew 11:21[55] in the New Testament. What items seem to represent mourning and regret?[T25]

- ▪
- ▪

Compare Jeremiah 31:19[51] with Luke 18:13-14.[56] What similar behaviors illustrate self-depreciation or self-reproach?

- ▪
- ▪

HISTORY & CULTURE:[T25]
SACKCLOTH AND ASHES—
Sackcloth was a coarse cloth, dark in color, usually made of goat's hair. It was worn by mourners and captives, sometimes over the top of regular clothing and sometimes next to the skin. Sackcloth was also worn in times of crying out to God in deep distress on behalf of the nation of Israel.

Wearing ashes, usually on the head, was an ancient Hebrew custom showing mourning or humiliation. Those who were deeply penitent or afflicted in some way would sit or wallow in ashes. When used figuratively, ashes signifies frailty, insignificance, and worthlessness. The expression "dust and ashes" was a Hebrew play on words. It signified man's origin and contrasted the lowliness of man with the dignity of God. (*The Zondervan Pictorial Bible Dictionary*, Merrill C. Tenney, general editor [Nashville: The Southwestern Company, 1974], p. 76.)

For further study:
Esther 3:13–4:4
Isaiah 22:12
Jeremiah 6:26

⁵⁶LUKE 18

13-14 "But the tax-gatherer, standing some distance away, was even unwilling to lift up his eyes to heaven, but was beating his breast, saying, 'God, be merciful to me, the sinner!' I [Jesus] tell you, this man went down to his house justified rather than the other; for everyone who exalts himself shall be humbled, but he who humbles himself shall be exalted."

⁵⁷ISAIAH 61

1-3 "The Spirit of the Lord GOD is upon me [Jesus], Because the LORD has anointed me To bring good news to the afflicted; He has sent me [Jesus] to bind up the broken-hearted, To proclaim liberty to captives, And freedom to prisoners; To proclaim the favorable year of the LORD, And the day of vengeance of our God; To comfort all who mourn, To grant those who mourn in Zion, Giving them [beauty] instead of ashes, The oil of gladness instead of mourning, The mantle of praise instead of a spirit of fainting. So they will be called oaks of righteousness, the planting of the LORD, that He may be glorified."

Sackcloth and ashes were worn to indicate mourning or utter humility. Beating one's breast or thigh shows grief and self-reproach. The idea of self-depreciation goes very much against conventional (earthly) wisdom today—even in the church. But in the Bible and in the early church, antidotes to pride were sought after by heroes of the faith. These godly men and women knew that true humility was necessary for coming to God. Repentance is more than just verbalizing a laundry list of sins. It incorporates being so sick of our sinfulness that we turn away from a lifestyle of sin, never to return to our former selves.

IN POVERTY OF SPIRIT

The Greek language has two words for "poor." One is the working poor who eke out a meager living. The other poor, *pto-chos*, refers to "one who crouches and cowers; helpless, beggarly." This is the word used in Matthew 5:3-4 when Jesus said, "Blessed are the poor *[pto-chos]* in spirit, for theirs is the kingdom of heaven. Blessed are those who mourn, for they shall be comforted."

If we would inherit the kingdom of heaven, we must come to the Lord in abject spiritual poverty, humbled by our own insufficiency, broken and mourning over our own depravity, and in awe of a God who would extend His mercy to us. If we would be filled with divine wisdom, we must be emptied of earthly delusion. We must repent in spiritual and emotional sackcloth and ashes. And we must turn!

When we are broken, we can claim the promises of Isaiah 61:1-3.⁵⁷ Read these verses in the adjacent column. Write down the promises you want to personally claim.

BRINGING IT HOME . . .

1. The Christian life begins with repentance that is a result of humility before God. If you are a Christian, it is important to be able to share your own story of repentance. If you have never done so, write out your testimony. Include what you were like before you knew Christ, what particular verse or scriptural truth made you thirsty for God, and what immediate and long-range changes took place in your life as a result of humbling yourself before God. Work on getting your story down to about three minutes so you will always be ready to share it.

2. This is a good time to look at your life in light of Isaiah 61:1-3.[T57] What are some of the things from which you need to be set free? Read "Point of Interest:[T26] Imaginary Gods" and answer the following questions:

   - What is your view of God?

   - What is the basis for that view?

   - How does that view compare with the God of the Bible?

POINT OF INTEREST:[T26]

IMAGINARY GODS—Left to our own devices, we create gods of our imagination, gods whom we can control and manipulate, gods who are projections of ourselves. The God of Scripture, however, is totally different from anything we would think up, totally *other* than what we imagine.

Yet the infinite (beyond limits) and transcendent (beyond comprehension) God took on human flesh and became utterly imminent (close to us) and involved in the human condition. In love He reached down to us. He reaches still.

At the point of salvation, God launches a process of gradual transformation, from the inside out, through the Holy Spirit. God intends to conform us to the image of Christ who is our picture of a life lived by divine wisdom. God will form and forge us toward Christlike character until we are conformed to His expectations, desires, and purposes for our lives.

DAILY READING
Read Proverbs 5:1-14. Mark the verse that stands out most to you today.

DAY 4

WISDOM AND THE SPIRIT

Wisdom involves fear of the Lord, humility, and repentance. Repentance includes confessing (agreeing with God that sin is sin) and mourning our sins as well as making a U-turn from our old ways of life. This is a tall order, one that goes against our nature. How, then, can we accomplish these prerequisites for divine wisdom? *We can't, of course. Our helplessness is why a merciful God provided us with His Spirit.* According to Acts 2:38,[58] how does one receive the Holy Spirit?

As promised, when we cry out to God and search for Him with all our heart, He dispatches the Holy Spirit to us; thus, God "is found by us" (Jeremiah 29:13-14[10]). The Spirit of God draws us into the secret places of God's heart and indwells the secret places of our hearts. There the Spirit of God begins to do a mighty work in our lives from the inside out. *There He seals us as a child of God forever.* (Read Ephesians 1:13-14.[59])

We've already seen the work of the Spirit in regard to wisdom in day 1 of this unit. Read Exodus 31:1-6[6] again. *To enable us to do the work to which He calls us, the Holy Spirit fills us with the attributes and abilities we need.* To enable Bezalel to work on the tabernacle, He gave wisdom, understanding, knowledge, and craftsmanship. Read Romans 15:13,[60] Micah 3:8,[61] and Galatians 5:22-23.[41] The Holy Spirit fills us with what other attributes?

God is concerned about our obedience. Read Ezekiel 36:27[62] and Galatians 5:16.[63] How does the Spirit contribute to our obedience?

---

[58] **ACTS 2**

38 Repent, and let each of you be baptized in the name of Jesus Christ for the forgiveness of your sins; and you shall receive the gift of the Holy Spirit.

[59] **EPHESIANS 1**

13-14 In Him, you also, after listening to the message of truth, . . . having also believed, you were sealed in Him with the Holy Spirit of promise . . . given as a pledge of our inheritance.

[60] **ROMANS 15**

13 Now may the God of hope fill you with all joy and peace in believing, that you may abound in hope by the power of the Holy Spirit.

[61] **MICAH 3**

8 I am filled with power— With the Spirit . . . with justice and courage.

[62] **EZEKIEL 36**

27 "I will put My Spirit within you and cause you to walk in My statutes, and you will be careful to observe My ordinances."

[63] **GALATIANS 5**

16 Walk by the Spirit, and you will not carry out the desire of the flesh.

[64] **1 THESSALONIANS 1**

5 For our gospel did not come to you in word only, but also in power and in the Holy Spirit and with full conviction.

God's instructions are revealed through His Word and through His Spirit. The first is by commandment. Commandment includes the absolutes of Scripture—God's "do's and dont's." They represent the boundaries of righteousness to be observed by all citizens who have sought amnesty in the kingdom of God. Crossing those boundaries constitutes clear violation of kingdom laws and brings sure (but not always swift) consequences.

Read the following statements and decide if each is true or false.

T F What one Christian can do with a clear conscience may be different from what his or her best friend may do.

T F One way to determine whether something (not addressed directly in Scripture) is right or wrong is to follow inner promptings.

T F There are times when a temptation is so strong that one has no choice but to give in.

T F Each Christian is responsible only for his or her own behavior.

T F Convictions are usually as strong as the temptation is imminent.

The Holy Spirit doesn't just *identify* boundaries. Read in 1 Thessalonians 1:5[64] how He also protects us. What work of the Spirit do you see in this Scripture?

When we begin to wander too close to a boundary of righteousness, *the Holy Spirit deals with us individually.* He troubles our spirits with an internal flutter or sense of warning or conviction.[T27] Unlike commandments, however, the boundaries of convictions may be more narrow for one person than for another.

Personal convictions are initiated in us by God to create a buffer zone between us and our own areas of weakness. Some need a wider hedge in the area of sexuality; others, in financial responsibility. (For example, a man may decide to stop watching football on television because he is convicted of putting sports above his family life. A woman may decide to stop shopping with friends because she is convicted of compulsive buying.)

POINT OF INTEREST:[T27]
CONVICTIONS are not absolutes of Scripture but are self-imposed resolutions or prohibitions prompted by the Spirit. They are meant to either draw us closer to God or keep us further away from temptations where we are personally vulnerable. Proverbs are helpful in forging certain convictions because they show us the ultimate consequences of behaviors that may seem innocent enough in the beginning. Many people have invalidated their testimony in ministry through small acts of compromise. We each have to discern what *we* can or cannot do and to remember that we can't trust the flesh!

Put an extra margin between yourself and whatever draws you into temptation. Remember, convictions are between you and God. Don't impose your vulnerabilities on others—they'll have enough of their own!

For further study:
John 16:8
Romans 14:13-14,22-23
1 Corinthinians 10:13

⁶⁵1 CORINTHIANS 2

9-10 "THINGS WHICH EYE HAS NOT SEEN AND EAR HAS NOT HEARD, [NOR] . . . ENTERED THE HEART OF MAN, ALL THAT GOD HAS PREPARED FOR THOSE WHO LOVE HIM." For to us God revealed them through the Spirit; for the Spirit searches all things, even the depths of God.

⁶⁶ROMANS 8

26 And in the same way the Spirit also helps our weakness; for we do not know how to pray as we should, but the Spirit Himself intercedes for us with groanings too deep for words.

⁶⁷1 CORINTHIANS 10

13 No temptation has overtaken you but such as is common to man; and God is faithful, who will not allow you to be tempted beyond what you are able, but with the temptation will provide the way of escape also, that you may be able to endure it.

Convictions may also be positive, such as daily Bible reading or prayer. The point is that the Holy Spirit knows us intimately and convicts us uniquely and protectively. He is a *personal* trainer.

The Holy Spirit has another role that we've mentioned in earlier excursions. Read 1 Corinthians 2:9-10.⁶⁵ What is another job of the Spirit as illustrated here?

The Spirit of truth (John 14:17) is the bearer of divine wisdom. The Spirit reveals things of God we've never seen, heard, nor even thought. The Spirit also reveals our purpose. The universal purpose for all Christians is, of course, the Great Commandment (to love God and others—Matthew 22:37-39) and the Great Commission (evangelism—Matthew 28:19-20). But God also has a specific purpose for each of us—one that unfolds as we meditate and mentally process our unique background, opportunities, training, gifts, and temperament. God reveals His purpose as we search Scripture, seek counsel, and pray for guidance. *So the Spirit reveals to us both the truths of God and His plan for our lives.* He then guides us toward that end.

The Spirit is always in touch with the limits of our humanity, and He runs interference on our behalf. Read Romans 8:26.⁶⁶ What does the Spirit do for us according to this verse?

We don't even know how to pray! But the Spirit is simultaneously in touch with us and with God. As we saw in 1 Corinthians 2:14-16,³¹ the Spirit knows the mind and the will of God. He knows our weaknesses as well. Therefore, *the Spirit appeals to the Father on our behalf for our highest good,* even when we don't have a clue about what we need.

What are five one-word summaries of the Holy Spirit's work in our lives? (Hint: See the italicized sentences; four out of these five verbs rhyme.)

-
-
-
-
-

Many other works of the Spirit lead us in wisdom—too many to name in this short excursion. However, a brief overview is provided in the Side Tours column.[T28]

BRINGING IT HOME . . .

1. Each of us has personal areas where the Spirit of God seems to more strictly constrain us or restrict us. What are some of those areas in your life? In other words, what are some of your areas of personal vulnerability?

2. Temptations that are *individually* problematic often are not just common weaknesses of the flesh but are residual longings for previously realized desires or lusts. Can you identify a "point of entry" that now makes you vulnerable to areas of potential sin? Do you cooperate with the Spirit on the boundaries of safety that God establishes for your life according to 1 Corinthians 10:13?[67] If not, how can you do so?

CROSS REFERENCES:[T28]

WORKS OF THE SPIRIT—
Nehemiah 9:20,30: instruction, admonishment
Isaiah 11:2: wisdom, understanding, counsel, strength, knowledge, and the fear of the Lord
Ezekiel 36:26: a new heart and a new spirit
John 3:3-5, 6:63: rebirth into the kingdom of God; eternal life
14:16-17,26: helper forever; truth; teacher, reminder
Acts 1:8,16: power for witnessing, missions; boldness; hope, love, resurrection
Romans 8:14,16: leading and guidance; confirmation of our salvation
14:17, 15:16: righteousness, peace, joy; sanctification
1 Corinthians 2:9-10: revelation of God's mysteries
12:3,7: ability to yield to God; spiritual gifts (words of wisdom and knowledge, faith, healing)
2 Corinthians 3:17, 13:14: liberty; fellowship
Galatians 3:3, 5:18: completion/perfection in Christ; freedom from the law
5:22-23: love, joy, peace, patience, kindness, goodness, faithfulness, gentleness, self-control
Ephesians 1:13, 4:3: sealed in Him (security); unity

DAILY READING
Read Proverbs 5:15-23. Mark the verse that stands out most to you today.

DAY 5

WISDOM IS A PERSON

[68]JOHN 7

37-38 Now on the last day . . . of the feast, Jesus stood and cried out, saying, "If any man is thirsty, let him come to Me and drink. He who believes in Me, as the Scripture said, 'From his innermost being shall flow rivers of living water.'"

[69]JOHN 10

10 "I came that they might have life, and might have it abundantly."

[70]THE GOSPELS

Matt. 9:35 And Jesus was going about all the cities and the villages, teaching. . . .

Mark 2:13 And He went out again by the seashore . . . teaching.

Luke 21:37 Now during the day He was teaching in the temple.

John 18:20 Jesus answered him, "I have spoken openly to the world; I always taught . . . where all the Jews come together; and I spoke nothing in secret."

For the one who fears the Lord, a humble, repentant heart creates an open door for the Spirit of God. The Spirit knows the heart of the Father and reveals to us the mind of Christ—our source of divine wisdom. But what do we know of wisdom itself? Begin today's study by reading Proverbs 8:1-33 in appendix A.

Proverbs describes wisdom using the imagery of a woman named Wisdom.[T29] Let's closely examine this persona and her works. Read Proverbs 1:22 and 8:4-5 again. To whom does Wisdom call?

No one is left out. Wisdom calls to everyone from the naive to the scoffer. Read Proverbs 1:20-21, 8:1-3, and 9:1-3. List the places from which Wisdom calls out to people.

What has she prepared for them?

There is no secrecy. Wisdom calls out openly to all people in common places and situations—from the marketplace and the streets to the places of the elite (including government) to feast at her banquet. She calls all to turn (or repent) at her reproof, acquire her, prize her, guard her, love her, embrace her, listen to her, heed her instruction, and watch for her daily. In response, she makes some awesome promises. Read the Proverbs listed below and write down some of the promises.

1:23

1:33

4:6-9

8:32-35

Read Proverbs 1:24-32 and 8:36. Wisdom issues a warning to those who refuse her call, neglect her counsel, ignore her reproof, hate knowledge, and do not fear the Lord, that is, she will:

- ▪
- ▪
- ▪
- ▪

Spurning Wisdom is foolish, not only because of the consequences but also because we fail to make use of her timeless resources. According to Proverbs 8:22-31, how long has Wisdom been available to humankind?

Wisdom was not only present at the beginning of creation but was always with God who has no beginning. At the creation of the cosmos, Wisdom was at the Creator's side, rejoicing in His works. Wisdom was also the embodiment of treasures that exceed the value of anything on earth because of the supreme gifts she embodies. Nothing that we can desire compares to Wisdom. Read Proverbs 3:13-26 and 8:6-21. Write some of Wisdom's resources and benefits below.

Wisdom offers us the freedom to reap the benefits of obedience. There is *no* earthly source of lasting peace, happiness, power, riches, honor, discretion, prudence, counsel, knowledge, or righteousness. But God has given us much more than a literary device (personification) for understanding wisdom. Let's compare the person of Wisdom in Proverbs with the person of Wisdom in the New Testament.

According to Proverbs, all people are called to eat and drink at Wisdom's banquet and to receive abundant life. Read John 7:37-38[68] and John 10:10.[69]

Who is calling and what is He offering?

In Proverbs, Wisdom proclaims openly from ordinary places. Read the verses from the Gospels.[70]

Who is teaching and from what specific places?

STUDY TECHNIQUE:[T29]

TYPES AND SHADOWS—Foreshadowing is an important concept when studying the Old Testament. Most events and characters are best understood as physical or literal representations of what would become a spiritual reality in Christ. Wisdom in Proverbs is a "type" that foreshadows Jesus. The relationship of the person Wisdom in Proverbs to Jesus is this: Jesus is wisdom incarnate (in the flesh); that is, Jesus personifies, personalizes, and humanizes God's wisdom. Jesus walks it out so we can see God's wisdom carried out in everyday affairs. For example, you may have noticed in Scripture that Jesus responded differently to different people. Those needing Him or truly seeking to learn from Him were met with kindness while the arrogant or those with hidden motives were rebuked. You see in Jesus One who knows the hearts of people so well that He doesn't entrust Himself to them. Yet He is never cynical and He continues to serve.

The furnishings of the tabernacle (see p. 23,[T8] "The Tabernacle") is one of the best examples of an Old Testament "type"—a shadow of what was to come in Christ.

71 ACTS 2

17 "And . . . in the last days," God says, . . . "I will pour forth of My Spirit upon all mankind."

72 ZECHARIAH 12

10 "And I will pour out on the house of David and on the inhabitants of Jerusalem, the Spirit of grace and of supplication, so that they will look on Me whom they have pierced."

73 JOHN 1

1-2,4,14 In the beginning was the Word, and the Word was with God, and the Word was God. He was in the beginning with God. . . . In Him was life, and the life was the light of men. . . . The Word became flesh, and dwelt among us, and we beheld His glory . . . full of grace and truth.

74 COLOSSIANS 1

15-18 He is the image of the invisible God, the firstborn of all creation. For by Him [Jesus] all things were created, both in the heavens and on earth . . . all things have been created by Him and for Him. . . . He is before all things, and in Him all things hold together. He is also head of the body, the church.

75 MATTHEW 13

45-46 "The kingdom of heaven is like a merchant seeking fine pearls, and upon finding one pearl of great value, he . . . sold all that he had, and bought it."

76 COLOSSIANS 2

2-3 The wealth . . . comes from . . . a true knowledge of God's mystery, that is, Christ Himself, in whom are hidden all the treasures of wisdom and knowledge.

In Proverbs, Wisdom promises to pour out her spirit on those who seek her and make her words known to them. Read Acts 2:17[71] and Zechariah 12:10.[72] Whose Spirit are these Scriptures talking about?

Wisdom was with God in the beginning and was involved in creation according to Proverbs. Read John 1:1-2,4,14[73] and Colossians 1:15-18.[74] Who was with God in the beginning? Who is the Creator?

Proverbs compares wisdom to jewels and tells us that Wisdom is more valuable than anything we can desire. Read Matthew 13:45-46[75] and Colossians 2:2-3.[76]

Who is the pearl of great price; the hidden mystery or treasure?

According to 1 Corinthians 1:24,30 the attributes of God—His integrity, righteousness, justice, faithfulness, holiness, goodness, love, and truth—become ours in Christ:

> But to those who are the called . . . Christ the power of God and the wisdom of God. . . . But by His doing you are in Christ Jesus, who became to us wisdom from God, and righteousness and sanctification, and redemption.[T30]

The *word* of wisdom personified in Proverbs became the *flesh* of wisdom—expressed, fulfilled, and embodied in Jesus. The One who created the universe emptied Himself of His deity and came to earth as a helpless baby and a humble, sacrificial lamb of God. He came that we might know Him. Do you?

BRINGING IT HOME . . .

The primary elements of salvation we've seen thus far are:

- receiving and believing God's truth about sin

- agreeing with God about our own sinfulness; confessing and mourning over our sin

- rejecting and turning from old ways of life

- trusting in Christ alone for His saving work and receiving His forgiveness

- accepting Christ as Lord and receiving the seal and assurance of His Holy Spirit, as demonstrated by an ever-increasing Christlikeness

Because they are taken directly from Scripture, each of our personal salvation experiences should reflect these elements, regardless of our religious backgrounds or our church affiliations. If your salvation experience doesn't reflect these elements, ask God to reveal the truth of your position—are you "in Him?"

1. Review the promises you've recorded (on page 68) from Proverbs 1:23,33; 4:6-9; and 8:32-35. Which of these promises of Wisdom is most meaningful to you? Why?

2. Have you truly committed your life to Christ and trusted in Him alone for forgiveness of sin? If not, review this study up to this point, talk to the leader of your study group, or seek out the pastor of a Christ-centered church in your area. If you are ready to receive Christ, turn to appendix B for some help. Then share your decision with someone who will be able to encourage the "new" you. This is the first major step in knowing truth.

   If so, praise God for His forgiveness and for giving you the "mind of Christ" as Paul wrote in 1 Corinthians 2:16. This means that if you are facing an important or difficult decision, you can count on Him to give you the wisdom to discern His will.

POINT OF INTEREST:[T30]
GOD IS SOVEREIGN—Behind all wisdom is the sovereignty of God. Our plans are at best tentative, temporary, disconnected from the needs of others, and often never realized. God's counsel and plans, which are permanent and have unity, cannot be thwarted by us or Satan. Because God's plans *will* be established, wisdom tells us to align ourselves with the things that will last, to desire what God desires for us because God's plans are holy and good—the best for us. Those who resist God's reign and rule should take warning! They will develop a calloused heart, a seared conscience, a deaf ear, a blind eye, and a hardened will against the convictions of God's Spirit. They are fools en route to becoming scoffers and reprobates. (Go back and review "reprobate" in unit 2, pages 46-49.)

DAILY READING
Read Proverbs 6:1-11 and mark the proverb that stands out most to you today. Review all the proverbs you marked this week and select one to memorize.

To the leader: For this session you will use the board or flipchart in activity 2.

1. God wants us to work hard and pursue excellence. He also tells us to avoid selfish ambition and sloth. As you are getting ready for group time to begin, decide whether each of the following people are examples of godly ambition or selfish ambition.
   A. *A young boy sacrifices most of his social life throughout his elementary and high school years to become the Tennis World Champion.*
   B. *A gifted girl competes ruthlessly, applies herself academically, and prepares by taking practice tests to achieve perfect scores on both the ACT and SAT exams and graduate as the valedictorian.*
   - How would your answers differ if you had the following facts?
   A. *The tennis champion is Michael Chang who prays before every match and verbally acknowledges Christ as his Savior and the power of prayer when interviewed (even by the secular press).*
   B. *This high school senior comes from a broken family and wants the opportunity to speak at her graduation and share how Christ changed her life and gave her hope and the ability to persevere even through hard family times.*
   - How can one differentiate between working toward excellence and selfish ambition?
   - Should a Christian ever want to improve his or her financial position? Or win at sports? Or excel academically?
   - When does ambition become selfish?

2. Think for a few moments about words or short phrases you would use to describe a humble person. Have each person in the group share one word or phrase and keep going around the room until no more new words are suggested. Write all of these words on a flipchart or board. Then read Philippians 2:1-11 aloud. Add any qualities your group missed.
   - What are the links between wisdom and humility and wisdom and pride?
   - How does humility relate to the "fear of the Lord" (Proverbs 1:7)?
   - Why is God so opposed to pride?

3. Before we can repent, we must recognize that we have broken God's standard. That is, we must agree with God that we are wrong. This is called confession. Then we are ready for repentence.
   - What are the two aspects of true repentence?
   - Which of these two aspects is easier for most people? Explain.
   - Often when people are stopped for speeding, they tell the officer, "I'm sorry." For what do you think they feel sorry? How can you tell if this is true repentance?

4. God knows we cannot live the Christian life in our own strength. Therefore He has given us His Spirit to indwell and empower us. The Holy Spirit ministers to us in many ways. This study has covered five specific ones: *seals our citizenship in God's kingdom; fills us with the mind of Christ; deals with our sin through convicton; reveals God's will and purpose for us; and appeals or intercedes in prayer to the Father for us.*
   - What is the result of each of these roles the Spirit plays? What difference do they make in your life?
   - Share specific examples from Scripture or your personal experiences of each role of the Spirit.
   - Which of these aspects of the Holy Spirit's work is most meaningful to you? Why?

5. Throughout our study we have been looking at biblical wisdom versus worldly folly. We also have seen that the *word* of wisdom personified in the book of Proverbs became the *flesh* of wisdom in the person of Jesus.
   - How does the book of Proverbs contrast the person of wisdom with the person of folly? Use verses from appendix A to support your answer.
   - In what specific ways does Jesus Christ perfectly reflect wisdom?

Close your group time with prayer. Have everyone pray for the person on his or her right (aloud or silently) asking God to give that person wisdom in the following areas: pursuit of excellence, humble spirit before God, open communication with God, submission to the Spirit's work, and application of wisdom.

INTRODUCTION TO UNIT 4
EMBRACING THE WORD

Destination: To gain a deeper appreciation of the Word of God so that it impacts all aspects of our thoughts and behavior.

God used the powerful influence of my godly grandfather to instill in me (Gail) an insatiable love of the Word. My grandfather literally wore out several large-print Bibles. Though he didn't come to Christ until his late fifties, his understanding of Scripture was both simple and profound; and even with his limited education, he could challenge me with intriguing questions. More importantly, my grandfather openly expressed his own deep love for Jesus.

Just like my grandfather, the more I read about Jesus, the more I love Him; and the more I love Him, the stronger my desire to know Him and to please Him. Grandfather's role in my life was the same as the role of the Proverbs father; namely, to instill in his child a love for the words of wisdom. Toward that end, the father speaks out passionately, entreating his son to embrace his teaching. The Proverbs father appeals to the son with matters of the heart as well as the mind, with relational as well as logical reasonings. Through ten mini-sermons in Proverbs 1–9, the father exhorts the son to value the words of wisdom, to hear them rightly, to apply his mind toward understanding them, to meditate on them, and to believe and obey them.

Unit 4 looks at the great worth of the Word of God by drawing parallels between the value of the whole counsel of God and the value placed on the words of wisdom according to the book of Proverbs. This unit will help us gain a greater appreciation for the Word of God that we, too, may more deeply value, hear, understand, meditate on, believe, and obey the words of the Father. Therefore, we join Paul in praying

> that you may be filled with the knowledge of His will in all spiritual wisdom and understanding, so that you may walk in a manner worthy of the Lord, . . . bearing fruit in every good work and increasing in the knowledge of God . . . joyously giving thanks to the Father, who has . . . transferred us to the kingdom of His beloved Son, in whom we have redemption, the forgiveness of sins. And He [Jesus] is the image of the invisible God, the first-born of all creation. For by Him all things were created, both in the heavens and on earth, visible and invisible, whether thrones or dominions or rulers or authorities. . . . And He is before all things, and in Him all things hold together. He is also head of the body, the church; and He is the beginning, the first-born from the dead; so that He Himself might come to have first place in everything. For it was the Father's good pleasure for all the fullness to dwell in Him, and through Him to reconcile all things to Himself, having made peace through the blood of His cross; through Him, I say, whether things on earth or things in heaven. And although you were formerly alienated and hostile in mind, engaged in evil deeds, yet He has now reconciled you in His fleshly body through death, in order to present you before Him holy and blameless and beyond reproach—if indeed you continue in the faith firmly established and steadfast, and not moved away from the hope of the gospel that you have heard, which was proclaimed in all creation under heaven. (Colossians. 1:9-23)

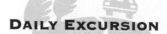
DAY 1

VALUING THE FATHER'S WORDS

[77] PSALM 78

5 For He established a testimony in Jacob, and appointed a law in Israel, which He commanded our fathers, that they should teach them to their children.

[78] DEUTERONOMY 6

6-7 And these words, which I am commanding you today, shall be on your heart; and you shall teach them diligently to your sons and shall talk of them when you sit in your house and when you walk by the way and when you lie down and when you rise up.

[79] JOHN 5

19 Jesus . . . was saying to them, ". . . the Son can do nothing of Himself, unless it is something He sees [God] the Father doing; for whatever the Father does, these things the Son also does in like manner."

The imagery that arises from reading Proverbs 1–9 is that of a father who is beginning to teach a naive, untutored child—one who has not yet formed a sense of prudence, discernment, equity, and righteousness. Read Psalm 78:5[77] and Deuteronomy 6:6-7[78] in the adjacent column and Proverbs 22:6 from appendix A.

Fathers were commanded to teach their children diligently as they sat, walked, laid down, and got up. The father in Proverbs is a living picture of the Deuteronomy father; that is, one who is continually teaching his son. The father is patient. He repeats many expressions, going back and forth as though attempting to cut furrows into his son's mind.[T32] Have you noticed some repetition in this study of Proverbs?[T33] Our goal, too, is to help you cut furrows deeply into your long-term memory so that your knowledge will remain.

THE FATHER'S GOAL

The goal of the father in Proverbs is to produce a wise man, one who will both hear and increase in learning (Proverbs 1:5). The father wants the son not only to be teachable and to listen—but also to take action. Read Proverbs 2:1-5. Match each verb phrase from column 1 to its application in column 2.

Column 1	Column 2
receive sayings	listen for truth
treasure commandments	pay attention/accept God's Word
make ear attentive	long for wisdom/desire truth
incline heart	wrestle with God for revelation
cry for discernment	pray fervently for understanding
lift voice for understanding	intently study God's Word
seek/search for wisdom	memorize Scripture/value God's Word

Proverbs 2:1-5 reveals the father's directive for active, eager participation by the son in attaining wisdom. The father does not desire his son to accept his words passively but rather to become involved in a white-hot

pursuit of wisdom! From appendix A, read Proverbs 1:8-9, 3:1-4, 4:7-9, and 6:20-21. What are the common threads in these verses?

The goal is not to fill the son's head with mere information or even knowledge. Instead, the father wants his words of wisdom to become bound to his son, written on his heart, adorning and gracing him so that they become integrated into his person. He wants his words to cause change in his son's life because he knows that *whatever words his son implants into his own heart and mind will wholly determine how he lives his life.*

Read Proverbs 4:1-13 (especially note verses 3-4 and 11). On what basis does the father appeal to the son in these verses?

The father reflects on his own experience when he was "the son." Because he received wisdom and learned obedience from *his* father, the Proverbs father offers his own life as an example—as one who has walked in obedience to his own father's words and experienced the benefits of wisdom. The Proverbs father, then, appeals to his son on the basis of his lineage; and he desires for the son to reflect and preserve the family's honor.

From Scripture it is clear that all people belong to one of two families. Read John 5:19[79] and John 8:44.[42]

Who are the two spiritual fathers from whom all character comes?

- ▪
- ▪

What will their children want to do, according to these verses?

- ▪
- ▪

Even though we are created by God, we are born with "bad blood." Because of the Fall as recorded in Genesis 3, all of us have inherited the sin nature of our father, the Devil. But Christ, through His death and

POINT OF INTEREST:[T32]

GODLY PARENTS PERPETUATE WISDOM by exhorting their children to pursue and embrace God's Word. The wisdom God offers to our children is the same wisdom He used to transform chaos into cosmos, to create and shape this world into a beautiful, ordered planet that is an exquisite design, even in its fallen state. In the same way, Proverbs shows us that God can take our children, with their own chaotic and unruly natures, and make their lives into something meaningful and profound.

This picture of the untutored child in Proverbs is consistent with the New Testament vision of people who are dead in their trespasses and sins, naturally without God in a fallen world and in need of redemption. The One who said, "Let there be light and life" on a darkened planet also says, "Let there be light and life" in our darkened hearts. His desire for our children and for us is that we discover and pursue a moral path by surrendering ourselves to God and to His claims on our lives.

For further study:
Romans 6:1-14
Ephesians 2:1-10

STUDY TECHNIQUE:[T33]

REPETITION AS A TEACHING DEVICE—Repetition is a fundamental technique used by educators today. In almost all cases, information needs to be repeated many times before the student or learner gets the idea. Studies have indicated that a grade school student must hear new information about thirty times before it "sticks" and *three hundred times* if the new information contradicts a previously learned fact. (Lecture by Ms. Brenda Murphy, Sail-Away Reading Program, June 1997, Knoxville, TN.)

[80] 1 PETER 1

3,23 God . . . has caused us to be born again . . . through the resurrection of Jesus Christ. . . . For you have been born again, not of seed which is perishable but imperishable . . . through the living and abiding word.

[81] 1 JOHN 3

9 No one who is born of God practices sin, because His seed abides in him; . . . he is born of God.

[82] JOHN 14

9 Jesus said . . . "He who has seen Me has seen the Father."

[83] HEBREWS 1

3 He [Jesus] is the radiance of His [God's] glory and the exact representation [charakter] of His nature.

[84] 2 CORINTHIANS 3

18 But we all, with unveiled face beholding as in a mirror the glory of the Lord, are being transformed into the same image [eikon] from glory to glory.

[85] COLOSSIANS 3

9 Since you laid aside the old self with its evil practices, and have put on the new self who is being renewed to a true knowledge according to the image of the One who created him.

[86] 1 CORINTHIANS 15

49 And just as we have borne the image of the earthy, we shall also bear the image of the heavenly.

resurrection, offers us His cleansing blood—like a "spiritual transfusion." Read 1 Peter 1:3,23[80] and 1 John 3:9.[81] What does God cause to happen to us through the resurrection of Jesus Christ?

In Christ, we are so fully adopted that we are reborn. God's imperishable seed is implanted in us, giving us a new lineage and a new nature that now reflects the image of a new Father. Read John 14:9,[82] Hebrews 1:3,[83] 2 Corinthians 3:18,[84] Colossians 3:9,[85] and 1 Corinthians 15:49.[86] Whose image does Jesus reflect perfectly?

Whose image does the Christian reflect increasingly?

Jesus is the *exact representation* of the Father. This Greek word (used nowhere else in Scripture) is *charakter*—"a tool for engraving, a stamp or dye." We are being transformed into an *eikon*—"an image, a likeness"—not yet into an exact reflection of the Father but into an ever-growing likeness of the Son. *This growing likeness is a hallmark of a true Christian!*

We said in the beginning of today's excursion that the imagery in Proverbs 1–9 is that of a father teaching his untutored son. Images can reveal more than one truth. Could the Proverbs father be an image (picture) of God the Father, God the Son, a father in the flesh, or a father in the faith?[T34] Think of the most godly Christian family man you know. Is he a father? Is he a son? Does he have children of the flesh? Of the faith? Does he bear the image of his Father? Do you see that same image in his children? What about you? Do you value, hear, understand, meditate on, believe, and obey your Father's Word?

BRINGING IT HOME . . .

1. Name at least three verbal lessons that have most positively affected the way you live. Who taught you these important truths? What action do you need to take to ensure these teachings get passed on to the next generation and beyond?

2. Our actions are the most powerful form of communication. Whose life has had the most positive impact on you and the way you live your life? If you have never taken the time to thank this person, call or write today. Whose life has had the most negative impact on you? Have you forgiven this person? If not, spend time in prayer asking God to give you the grace and courage to do so.

3. Review the list of directives given by the father in Proverbs 2:1-5 concerning the importance of his words and their spiritual counterparts. Ask God to help you honestly and accurately rate yourself on each activity. Use a scale of 1 to 5 (1 means "I hardly ever do this" and 5 means "I do this on a consistent basis"). For any instructions you are not consistently following, what hinders you? Choose one activity where you need improvement and determine what you need to do (beginning today) to get past the hindrances.

LANGUAGE & LIT:[T34]
IMAGERY—The Bible often makes use of imagery, particularly in the books of the prophets, the book of Proverbs, and the parables of Jesus. Imagery is a literary device that uses words to call forth mental images or pictures in the imagination. Imagery often applies to more than one principle. Detecting the multiple levels requires pondering the images with acuity or discernment and praying for revelation of truth. The Proverbs father is an excellent example of multiple-level imagery.

DAILY READING
Read Proverbs 6:12-19. Mark the verse that stands out most to you today.

DAY 2

HEARING THE WORD

As you have been reading through the first nine chapters of Proverbs, you no doubt have noticed how often the father says, "listen," "hear," "incline your ear," "pay attention," "don't forget." The father seems to know well that his words may be lost to competing messages—distractions of life; demands of time; and (even worse) denial, rationalization,[T35] and self-justification. It takes effort to really hear the Word of God, for hearing is more than just allowing sound waves to pass through the auditory system. *Listening* is an action verb, an effort that includes both the mind and the will.

One of the most well-known parables of Jesus has to do with hearing the Word. Read Mark 4:2-3.[87] How does Jesus begin this parable?

Listen (hear) and behold (see). Like the Proverbs father, Jesus knew the importance of engaging the minds of His listeners before giving them His words of wisdom. Now, read Mark 4:3-9 below.

> "Behold the sower went out to sow; and . . . as he was sowing, some seed fell beside the road and the birds came and ate it up. And other seed fell on the rocky ground where it did not have much soil; and immediately it sprang up because it had no depth of soil. And after the sun had risen, it was scorched; and because it had no root, it withered away. And other seed fell among the thorns, and the thorns came up and choked it, and it yielded no crop. And other seeds fell into the good soil and as they grew up and increased, they yielded a crop and produced thirty, sixty, and a hundredfold." And He was saying, "He who has ears to hear, let him hear."

Who does Jesus say should hear the message of this parable?[T36]

Read John 8:47.[88] What does it take to have "ears that hear" the Word?

---

[87] MARK 4

2-3 And He was teaching them many things in parables, and was saying . . . "Listen . . . ! Behold."

[88] JOHN 8

47 "He who is of God hears the words of God; for this reason you do not hear them, because you are not of God."

[89] ROMANS 10

14,17 How then shall they call upon Him in whom they have not believed? And how shall they believe in Him whom they have not heard? And how shall they hear without a preacher? . . . So faith comes from hearing, and hearing by the word of Christ.

[90] GALATIANS 3

2 Did you receive the Spirit by the . . . Law, or by hearing with faith?

[91] ISAIAH 55

10-11 "For as the rain and the snow come down from heaven, And do not return there without watering the earth, And making it bear and sprout, And furnishing seed to the sower and bread to the eater; So shall My word be which goes forth from My mouth; It shall not return to Me empty, Without accomplishing what I desire, And without succeeding in the matter for which I sent it."

[92] 1 THESSALONIANS 2

13 You accepted it . . . [as] the word of God, which also performs its work in you who believe.

We've already seen from other Scriptures (such as 1 Corinthians 2:14-16[31]) that we cannot discern truth on our own. *Truth cannot be gained apart from a right relationship with the Source of truth* because God's Word is revealed to us by His Spirit. To hear God, then, we must be "of God," meaning "born again." Read again 1 Peter 1:23.[80]

We are born again of imperishable seed through *hearing* the living and abiding Word. This brings us to an interesting question and seeming paradox. If we aren't able to really hear God's Word until we are "of God," how can we ever become His? Paul addresses this question in Romans 10:14,17[89] and Galatians 3:2.[90]

How does faith come?

How does the Spirit come?

Just *hearing* the Word of the Father opens up the doors to faith, and *hearing with faith* allows us to receive the Spirit of truth. How can mere words be so powerful? Read Isaiah 55:10-11[91] and 1 Thessalonians 2:13.[92]

What is going forth?

What will it do (and/or not do)?

God's power is resident in His Word—wisdom that had gone forth from the foundation of the earth (John 1:1-2,4,14[73] and Proverbs 8:22). His wisdom continues to go forth today, from Scripture and through His messengers as they preach, teach, share, and live His Word.

The relationship between the Word and faith reveals the importance of proclaiming words of life to a dying world. It also highlights the importance of studying the Word so that we are able to share it accurately. Yet ours is not the only voice that proclaims the gospel.

POINT OF INTEREST:[T35]

RATIONALIZATION—There is something very distorted in human thinking. As a result of our fallen nature, we continually delude ourselves, rationalizing our positions, our decisions, and our disobedience. Scripture warns us that there is a way that seems right to us, but the end thereof is death (Proverbs 14:12). Therefore, we need an objective body of revelation and truth against which we can judge ourselves. We are not the standard; and while we may deceive ourselves, we really don't hide our true character from God nor from others. Proverbs 27:19 says, "as in water, face reflects face, so the heart of man reflects man." The fact is, our true character will eventually come out, and everyone, especially God, will observe it all.

CROSS REFERENCES:[T36]
WHO IS TO HEAR THE WORD OF THE LORD—
Isaiah 1:10: "You rulers"
66:5: "You who tremble at His word"
Jeremiah 19:3: "O kings of Judah"
22:29: "O land, land, land"
31:10: "O nations"
44:24: "All the people"
Ezekiel 34:7: "You shepherds"
Amos 3:1: "Sons of Israel"

93 ROMANS 1

18-20 For the wrath of God is revealed from heaven against all ungodliness and unright-eousness of men, who suppress the truth in unrighteousness, because that which is known about God is evident within them; for God made it evident to them. For since the creation of the world His invisible attributes, His eternal power and divine nature, have been clearly seen, being understood through what has been made, so that they are without excuse.

94 ROMANS 2

14-16 For when Gentiles who do not have the Law do instinctively the things of the Law, these, not having the Law, are a law to themselves, in that they show the work of the Law written in their hearts, their conscience bearing witness, and their thoughts alternately accusing or else defending them.

95 ISAIAH 46

9-11 "Remember the former things long past; For I am God and there is no other; I am God, and there is no one like Me; Declaring the end from the beginning and from ancient times, things which have not been done, saying, 'My purpose will be established, and I will accomplish all My good pleas-ure'; Calling a bird of prey from the east, the man of My pur-pose from a far country. Truly I have spoken; truly I will bring it to pass. I have planned it, surely I will do it."

Read Romans 1:18-20[93] and Romans 2:14-16.[94] Besides the Scriptures and our spoken word, how does God communicate with people?

-
-

What are the implications of this truth in relation to the gospel and salvation?

No one will be able to stand before God and say, "I never heard of you," because of creation and human con-science. God has placed His message all around us and within us. Remember the promise we saw in Jeremiah 29:13-14?[10] If we will seek Him, He will be found by us. God gives us assurance of His power to keep that prom-ise in Isaiah 46:9-11.[95] What will be brought to pass?

-
-

God did not make the knowledge of Himself depen-dent upon any human effort. Yet He has given us the incredible privilege of participating in the only activity that will have eternal consequences—sharing the gospel! So listen. Hear. Incline your ear. Pay attention. Stay in the Word. Don't forget. Then join the heavens in telling the glories of God.

BRINGING IT HOME . . .

1. Review today's study and list what you have learned about God's Word. Which of these truths impact(s) you the most at this point in your life? For what reasons? What specific Scriptures have impacted you for change during this journey toward wisdom? In what ways?

2. God tells us that "faith comes from hearing, and hearing by the word of Christ" (Romans 10:17). Besides this study, from what sources are you hearing God's Word? What other messages are you listening to on a regular basis? What changes, if any, do you need to make to assure you are not drowning out His voice?

3. A question that often comes up about the Christian faith and Jesus being the only way to God is: What about the person who never sees a Bible or hears a sermon about Christ? In light of Romans 1:18-20, how would you respond to this question? What attributes of God do you see revealed in His creation? How can you use this information when sharing the gospel?

DAILY READING

Read Proverbs 6:20-29. Mark the verse that stands out most to you today.

DAY 3

UNDERSTANDING THE WORD

[96]**MATTHEW 13**

18-23 "Hear then the parable of the sower.

"When anyone hears the word of the kingdom and does not understand it, the evil one comes and snatches away what has been sown in his heart. This is the one on whom seed was sown beside the road.

"And the one on whom seed was sown on the rocky places, this is the man who hears the word, and immediately receives it with joy; yet he has no firm root in himself, but is only temporary, and when affliction or persecution arises because of the word, immediately he falls away.

"And the one on whom seed was sown among the thorns, this is the man who hears the word, and the worry of the world, and the deceitfulness of riches choke the word, and it becomes unfruitful.

"And the one on whom seed was sown on the good soil, this is the man who hears the word and understands [sunemi] it; who indeed bears fruit, and brings forth, some a hundredfold, some sixty, and some thirty."

On day 2, we looked at many exhortations by the father, telling the son to listen, hear, and pay attention to his words. But getting the son's attention is obviously not the father's goal; it is the means, not the end. Likewise, the father's goal in these preparatory chapters is not to convey wisdom (though he does some of that), but to convey the *value* of wisdom. The father knows that if the son ever comprehends wisdom's immeasurable worth, he will then listen and strive to understand on his own initiative.[T37]

We also looked at the first part of the parable of the sower. Turn back to page 78 and read this parable from Mark's gospel. Now read it from Matthew 13:18-23[96] as Jesus explains this parable to His disciples.

In Luke 8:11 Jesus tells us that the "seed" in this parable is the Word of God. We see from the Scriptures that hearing—active listening and receiving of information—is a necessary *but insufficient* reaction to God's Word. In this parable, Jesus gives four different responses to the Word. Briefly describe the responses after hearing the Word:

Response   Result

1. _____
2. _____
3. _____
4. _____

Read Proverbs 2:1-5. After telling his son to receive, treasure, and pay attention to his words of wisdom, the father tells him to (complete the phrases below):

- incline his heart to:

- lift up his voice for:

The Hebrew word for "understanding," *tebunah,* used in Proverbs 2:1-5 and the Greek word *sunemi,* used in the parable of the sower have similar connotations. To appreciate the nuances of these words, let's first look at two uses of *tebunah.*

Tebunah originates from the root word *bin*, which means "to diligently consider, discern, investigate." But *tebunah* is used especially to denote either an act of wisdom (such as "by wisdom, God stretched out the heavens") or an involvement of a faculty (that is, incline "ear," lift "voice," "walk" straight.) *Tebunah* involves the mind and is translated "reasonings" in some texts. To see how this concept is used in Scripture, read Isaiah 44:9,14,15,17,19-20 below.

> Those who fashion a graven image are all of them futile, and their precious things are of no profit. . . . [A man] takes a cypress or an oak, and raises it for himself among the trees of the forest. . . . Then it becomes something for a man to burn, so he takes one of them and warms himself; he also makes a fire to bake bread. He also makes a god and worships it; he makes it a graven image, and falls down before it. . . . He also prays to it and says, "Deliver me, for thou art my god.". . . And no one recalls, nor is there knowledge or understanding [*tebunah*] to say, "I have burned half of it in the fire, and also have baked bread over its coals. I roast meat and eat it. Then I make the rest of it into an abomination, I fall down before a block of wood!". . . A deceived heart has turned him aside. And he cannot deliver himself, nor say, "Is there not a lie in my right hand?"

Do you see how *tebunah* is used to demonstrate deductive reasoning and logic? Here Isaiah critically analyzed the absurdity of worshipping an idol made by the worshiper. *Tebunah*, then, is a word whose fullest meaning involves both mental reasoning and physical response or action.

This same concept is used in the parable of the sower. In this case the Greek word for understanding, *sunemi*, is used. Reread Matthew 13:18-23, to see how this parable relates to understanding. Based on this passage:

On how many different types of soils were the seeds sown?

How many of these soils took in the seed?

POINT OF INTEREST:[T37]

KEEP GIVING THE GOSPEL—When you give the gospel to first-time hearers, they usually respond as if you've spoken in a foreign language. Before people begin to clue in, they must hear the story again and again—often from different people—because the message goes against the natural bent of human thinking. Personal merit or earning eternal life by keeping the law makes much more worldly sense than does "by grace through faith." Yet if anything is clear in Scripture, it is that the best of us don't deserve salvation, and that keeping the law is humanly impossible.

Faith in the Lord alone brings about justification. Faith releases God's power to work in our lives, enabling us to keep the law. Faith comes by hearing! And hearing! And hearing! Keep praying and keep giving out God's message of hope.

⁹⁷ MATTHEW 13

11-15 And He answered [His disciples] and said to them, "To you it has been granted to know the mysteries of the kingdom of heaven, but to them it has not been granted. For whoever has, to him shall *more* be given, and he shall have an abundance; but whoever does not have, even what he has shall be taken away from him. Therefore I speak to them in parables; because while seeing they do not see, and while hearing they do not hear, nor do they understand. And in their case the prophecy of Isaiah is being fulfilled, which says, 'YOU WILL KEEP ON HEARING, BUT WILL NOT UNDERSTAND; AND YOU WILL KEEP ON SEEING, BUT WILL NOT PERCEIVE; FOR THE HEART OF THIS PEOPLE HAS BECOME DULL, AND WITH THEIR EARS THEY SCARCELY HEAR, AND THEY HAVE CLOSED THEIR EYES LEST THEY SHOULD SEE WITH THEIR EYES, AND HEAR WITH THEIR EARS, AND UNDERSTAND WITH THEIR HEART AND RETURN, AND I SHOULD HEAL THEM.'"

How many soils produced lasting fruit?

Look at the four people represented by the different soils. One heard the Word only. The other three both heard and took in the Word. But only one yielded *abundant* fruit.

What did the fourth person do differently than the first three?

The fourth person not only heard, but also understood—*sunemi*. *Sunemi* strictly denotes collecting single features of an object and bringing them together into a whole—like working a puzzle or cultivating a garden. Mentally, it means to put it all together and make sense of it; to subject it to logic and analysis; to reason. Both the Hebrew *tebunah* and the Greek *sunemi* go beyond basic comprehension. Both of these words mean to be able to come to deeper understanding through reason.[T38]

In reading the parable of the sower, we usually credit the high yield of the seed to the soil. And soil is important! In Luke's Gospel we are told that the good soil is "an honest and good heart" (8:15). But even good soil is barren without *seed*—the Word. (Review Isaiah 55:10-11.[91])

Let's look at the larger context of the parable of the sower. Read Matthew 13:11-15.[97] Those who had been given a possession were going to receive more of it in abundance; those who didn't possess [in abundance] were going to lose what little they had. What is this possession?

The disciples possessed knowledge of "the mysteries of the kingdom of heaven" (verse 11). The losers "had not" because they didn't cultivate what they possessed; they didn't direct their faculties—ears, eyes, heart, mind—toward understanding. Review Proverbs 1:20–2:10 from appendix A. In these verses Wisdom called out. Her words were sown. But the hearers were deliberately blind, dumb, deaf, and disinterested. According to Matthew 13, without cultivation, limited revelation eventually will be blown

away, dried up, eroded, or choked out. Only the foolish will fail to cultivate the Word in their lives.

BRINGING IT HOME . . .

We learned in today's study that we can hear and even receive the Word without really understanding the Word. We also learned that understanding the Word requires reasoning through it and subjecting it to analysis, under the direction of the Holy Spirit.

1. Carefully analyze the spiritual conditions of the heart as represented by the four soils. Which soil are you?

2. Have you applied your reasoning abilities to the claims of the gospel? In what ways are you cultivating the knowledge that you have of the mysteries of the kingdom of heaven? Are you ready to give an account of the hope within you? Could you explain salvation by grace through faith in Christ to an unsaved friend or neighbor? What key concepts and verses would you share? (If you need help, refer to the plan of salvation provided in appendix B.)

POINT OF INTEREST:[T38]

HUMAN INTELLECT AND THE WORD OF GOD—We cannot attain God through human intellect. Yet God is pleased when we, in submission and dependence upon the Holy Spirit, apply our reasoning abilities to understanding His Word. In fact, God's messengers gave the gospel not as "pie in the sky," but by *reasoning* through the Scriptures.

Acts 17:1-3 tells us that "they came to Thessalonica, where there was a synagogue of the Jews. And according to Paul's custom, he went to them, and for three Sabbaths reasoned with them from the Scriptures, explaining and giving evidence that the Christ had to suffer and rise again from the dead, and saying, 'This Jesus whom I am proclaiming to you is the Christ.'"

God does not expect us to believe a nonsense message. Instead, He has given us a Word that will inspire, enlighten, and stimulate our thinking throughout our lives.

For further study:
Acts 17:10-12

DAILY READING

Read Proverbs 6:30-35. Mark the verse that stands out most to you today.

DAY 4

MEDITATING ON AND MEMORIZING THE WORD

As part of the exhortations in chapters 1–9, the Proverbs father tells his son to "treasure my commandments" (2:1 and 7:1); to "let your heart keep my commandments" (3:1); and to "keep [my words] in the midst of your heart" (4:21).

These questions are important: Do you read the Bible? Do you memorize it? Do you study it? Do you pray? If you don't do these things regularly, it's going to be very difficult for you to walk in wisdom. Many find it especially difficult to meditate on and memorize Scripture, yet this is vitally important. Simply reading Scripture each day and hearing a thirty-minute sermon each week is not enough.[T39] Perceiving or understanding truth *requires* that you think about and reason through the words you read. You must ask yourself: "What do these words mean?" and "How do they apply to my life?"

Read Proverbs 2:3-5,9-11; 4:20-22; and 6:22-23. What are some additional benefits or discernments associated with meditating on God's Word?

Read Joshua 1:8,[98] Psalm 1:1-3,[99] and 1 Chronicles 22:11-13.[100] How often should we meditate on the Word of God?

What is the reward for meditating on and obeying God's Word?

In the Hebrew, "meditate" is *hagah*, meaning "to moan, muse, or ponder." It conveys an idea of wrestling with an issue or concept to achieve understanding. In the Old Testament, there are often material rewards associated with meditating on and obeying the Word of God. But as we mentioned before, characters and events recorded in the Old Testament are often physical representations of what will become a spiritual reality in Christ (that is, a basic precept of Christianity). What

---

[98] **JOSHUA 1**

8 This book of the law shall not depart from your mouth, but you shall meditate *[hagah]* on it day and night, so that you may be careful to do according to all that is written in it; for then you will make your way prosperous, and then you will have success.

[99] **PSALM 1**

1-3 How blessed is the man who . . . [delights] in the law of the LORD, And in His law he meditates day and night. And he will be like a tree firmly planted by streams of water, Which yields its fruit in its season, And its leaf does not wither; And in whatever he does, he prospers *[euodoo]*.

[100] **1 CHRONICLES 22**

11-13 Now, my son, the LORD be with you that you may be successful . . . [and] keep the law of the LORD your God. Then you shall prosper, if you are careful to observe the statutes and the ordinances which the LORD commanded.

[101] **3 JOHN**

2 Beloved, I pray that in all respects you may prosper and be in good health, just as your soul prospers.

[102] **JAMES 1**

21 Therefore putting aside all filthiness and all that remains of wickedness, in humility receive the word implanted *[emphutos]*, which is able to save your souls.

might Old Testament material prosperity and wordly success be representing in the New Covenant kingdom of God? (Read 3 John 2.[101])

Wisdom in Proverbs mentions wealth, health, and honor as rewards for those who seek her and heed her words. However, as we've seen before, wisdom's greater blessings are not material. Write some of the spiritual blessings of wisdom from the following verses from Proverbs.

3:21-26

4:10

4:20-22

In Christ, there is no correlation between meditating on and obeying God's Word with material prosperity and worldly success. Instead, His rewards (like wisdom's) are far superior: spiritual growth, peace, and security—even in the midst of physical poverty or deprivation. Meditating on the Word of God causes our relationships, mental health, and emotional being to prosper. Most importantly, however, it causes our souls to prosper! The Greek word for "prosper" in 3 John 2 is *euodoo*, which means "a successful journey." Our souls prosper now and when our journey ends in eternal life with the Lord!

On our last excursion we learned from the parable of the sower that the seed (the Word of God) fell on four soils, each representing a condition of the human heart. But fruit came only from the seed that fell on good soil; that is, the heart that was prepared to both *receive* and *understand* (plant and cultivate) the seed. Read James 1:21.[102]

To receive the Word, what must we put away?

What attitude must we have?

What is the Word able to do?

How is the Word to be taken in (received)?

POINT OF INTEREST:[T39]

THE COST OF MEDITATION— In our society one of the hindrances to wisdom is having time to really think through issues. Our fast pace and the demands on our time make it difficult to relate to one another, much less to meditate. To add to the problem, most of us have developed poor ways of unwinding. Rather than improve ourselves with scriptural meditation and physical recreation, we amuse ourselves. We "zone out" in front of our TVs, for example, while precious moments sift through our fingers.

If we expect to grow in the Lord, we must be willing to ponder over His Word and to reason through His precepts. This takes time, and time is our most rapidly diminishing resource. If we value wisdom, however, time is a price we'll be willing to pay.

¹⁰³JOHN 8

31 Jesus therefore was saying to those Jews who had believed Him, "If you abide in My word, then you are truly disciples of Mine."

¹⁰⁴PSALM 119

11 Thy word I have treasured in my heart, that I may not sin against Thee.

¹⁰⁵ROMANS 10

8 "THE WORD IS NEAR YOU, IN YOUR MOUTH AND IN YOUR HEART"—that is, the word of faith which we are preaching.

¹⁰⁶HEBREWS 8

6 But now He has obtained a more excellent ministry, by as much as He is also the mediator of a better covenant, which has been enacted on better promises.

"Implanted" *[emphutos]* comes from the Greek root word *phuo*, which means "to bring forth; to produce." When we hear and meditate on Scripture, we are implanting and cultivating the Word. This will bring forth spiritual fruit in our lives just as surely as physical seeds in good soil will bring forth plant growth. We may not understand either process, but we cannot deny the results. So . . . is it necessary to memorize the Word for it to be implanted?

Read John 8:31,[103] Psalm 119:11,[104] and Romans 10:8.[105] What do you think? Why, or why not?

Meditating on Scripture keeps us from sin. It also prepares us to know how to share the Word with others. Review 1 Thessalonians 2:13[92] and then read the verses below.

1 Peter 3:15: Sanctify Christ as Lord in your hearts, always being ready to make a defense to everyone who asks you to give an account for the hope that is in you.

2 Timothy 2:15: Be diligent to present yourself approved to God as a workman who does not need to be ashamed, handling accurately the word of truth.

We are commanded to meditate on and to give out the Word, but we are not commanded (at least not directly) to memorize Scripture. The fact is, however, that memorization *happens* as a result of meditation; and Scripture memory always rewards the Christian![T40] Deliberate memorization speeds up the process of hiding the Word in our hearts.

Abiding in the Word is another hallmark of a true disciple of Christ. Be sure you aren't skipping the memory exercise at the end of each unit.

BRINGING IT HOME . . .

1. Honestly evaluate the amount of time you spend in God's Word each day (include your Bible study preparation and group time as well as your church attendance). Tally the hours per week. What grade would you expect if you spent this same amount of time and concentration on a college course? What would your Father think of your report card? What adjustments do you need to make?

2. In His Sermon on the Mount (specifically Matthew 6:28-34), Jesus tells us that God will meet our needs if we will seek His kingdom. But Jesus never, under the New Covenant, promised us material wealth or worldly success. In fact, He often pointed to those things (considered a sign of God's blessing under the Old Covenant) as causes for stumbling. Hebrews 8:6[106] tells us that the New Covenant is better than the Old for it is based on better promises. How do you see and reconcile these truths?

3. Our minds are always thinking about something. List some of the thoughts or topics that your mind gravitates to during your "down" times. Begin to train your mind to mediate on God's Word by reviewing the verses you have been memorizing.

POINT OF INTEREST:[T40]

PEACE FROM KNOWING THE WORD—Proverbs 3:16-21 tells us that keeping the words of wisdom brings peace. When you lie down you won't be afraid, your sleep will be sweet.

Some of us worry a lot when we go to sleep. That's a good index of whether or not we are meditating on the Word until its truths have begun to take hold of our thinking. Worry tells us that we're still trying to run our own lives and that we really don't trust God in those anxiety areas of our lives.

Catch yourself as you go to sleep. What are you anxious about? Let your emotions be a diagnostic tool to help you pinpoint those areas that are not yet yielded to God. Memorize Scripture that applies directly to that situation. When worries begin to rob you of sweet sleep, meditate on those Scriptures. Remember, Jesus says to give Him your heavy burdens. Remember, too, that God is in control (not you), and you can trust Him entirely, exclusively, and extensively. Read these Scriptures as needed in relation to:
- Fear: Matthew 10:29-31; Romans 8:5
- Love: John 15:9-14
- Money: Matthew 6:24-34
- Peace: John 14:25-27

For further study:
Psalms 63:6, 77:6, 119:15, 143:5, 145:5

DAILY READING
Read Proverbs 7:1-27. Mark the verse that stands out most to you today.

DAY 5

BELIEVING AND OBEYING THE WORD

107 LUKE 11

28 But He [Jesus] said, " . . . blessed are those who hear the word of God, and observe it."

108 JAMES 1

22,25 But prove yourselves doers of the word, and not merely hearers who delude themselves. . . . But one who looks intently at the perfect law . . . and abides by it, not having become a forgetful hearer but an effectual doer, this man shall be blessed in what he does.

109 2 THESSALONIANS 1

7-9 Jesus shall be revealed from heaven with His mighty angels in flaming fire, dealing out retribution to those who do not know God and to those who do not obey the gospel of our Lord Jesus. And these will pay the penalty of eternal destruction, away from the presence of the Lord.

At one time the Bible was little more to me (Gail) than a collection of great literature. I inherited the family respect for it, and I absorbed much of the Word from being taken consistently to church. As an adult, I read through the Bible several times, and my analytical mind would ponder over verses, attempting to put pieces together. I valued the Word, I heard the Word, I memorized the Word, and on a human level, I understood the Word. But I didn't obey it. Isn't that odd?

Perhaps you've also found it odd that there were no commands to *obey* in the first nine chapters of Proverbs. Obedience is there, of course, but not in plain English. The call to obedience is encompassed in the meaning of the word "hear;" that is, both to hear and heed. The kind of hearing the father wanted from his son is defined by the Hebrew word *shama. Shama* is translated "to continually listen, to comprehend," *and* "to completely and diligently obey." Let's look at obedience in the New Testament in Luke 11:28[107] and James 1:22,25.[108] What do the "blessed" have in common?

■

■

The father desires that the son be blessed! The father wants his son to avoid the consequences and pain of disobedience to wisdom principles. This is the very reason he is teaching his son in advance to hear and obey his words.

The disregard for God's Word in Genesis 3 bears consequences, even for us today. Read 2 Thessalonians 1:7-9.[109]

Who will be subject to retribution?

What is the ultimate consequence of disobedience?

Obedience is an action we take for the purpose of reaching some desirable goal or avoiding some

undesirable end. The motivation to either obey or disobey is directly related to (1) the intensity of our desire to achieve or avoid something and (2) the degree of certainty (belief) that our obedience will make a difference.

Suppose your employer requests that you be at work by 8:00 A.M. What might motivate you to show up on time?

- Desire

- Belief

Why might you decide it doesn't matter if you show up at the stroke of eight o'clock?

- Desire

- Belief

Your answers likely relate to the intensity of your desire for your paycheck and the degree to which you believe tardiness would impact your job. The spiritual point is this: Obedience is contrary to our rebellious sin nature. Therefore, behind *every* willful, human-centered act of obedience, there is *always* a self-serving motive—from survival to success, from longing to love. And behind every willful act of disobedience, there is either disinterest or disbelief in the associated rewards or consequences.

How could I (and others) disobey a Word that is valued, heard, understood, and even memorized?[T41] Or why would we consistently disregard the commandments of an all-powerful, all-knowing, ever-present, Holy God before whom we will one day give an account?

There are only two possible reasons: Either we don't believe what the Word says of the consequences or we don't care. (Only one of these makes sense. Believing but not caring about the consequences of disobedience would certainly draw question to our sanity!)

Scripture agrees. Read James 1:22,25,[108] again. "Merely hearers" are those who do what?

POINT OF INTEREST:[T41]
OBEDIENCE AND SALVATION—
Before I (Gail) became a Christian, I had a well-developed religious habit. Except for the occasional doubt in the pit of my stomach, I *believed* that I believed. But my lack of obedience and rebellion revealed a different story—a truth that for years I would deny. In His mercy, however, God finally used pain and poverty of spirit to break through my denial and to bring my rebellion to an end. I had not known Him. But at the point I truly believed, I obeyed. Perfectly? No. But increasingly, without rebellion, and with a deep desire to please my Lord.

¹¹⁰ MATTHEW 7

26-27 "And everyone who hears [akouo] these words of Mine, and does not act upon them, will be like a foolish man, who built his house upon the sand. And the rain descended, and the floods came, and the winds blew, and burst against that house; and it fell, and great was its fall."

¹¹¹ JOHN 1

12 But as many as received Him, to them He gave the right to become children of God, even to those who believe [pisteuo] in His name.

¹¹² MARK 12

29-31 Jesus answered . . . "'YOU SHALL LOVE THE LORD YOUR GOD WITH ALL YOUR HEART, AND WITH ALL YOUR SOUL, AND WITH ALL YOUR MIND, AND WITH ALL YOUR STRENGTH. . . . YOU SHALL LOVE YOUR NEIGHBOR AS YOURSELF.' There is no other commandment greater than these."

¹¹³ JOHN 14

15 "If you love Me, you will keep My commandments."

Read Matthew 7:26-27.¹¹⁰ To whom does Jesus compare the one who hears and does not act upon His Word?

When we reason through this issue, we can agree that it is beyond foolishness to knowingly receive the Word of Almighty God and not act on it. Therefore, deliberate, continual disobedience is a pretty reliable indicator that we really *don't* believe. Let's look at the concept of true belief from the Scriptures.

The Proverbs father called his son to *shama*—to continually hear, comprehend, and apply his will toward complete obedience. In the Greek, Jesus calls us to both *akouo*—"to hear and observe the facts objectively" and to *pisteuo*—"to believe; to both give intellectual assent and to entrust."

The New Testament concept of belief also includes the idea of receiving. Read John 1:12.¹¹¹ The Greek word *pisteuo* in John 1:12 carries the concept beyond believing about or even believing in the Word or Christ. It's a faith that takes us out of ourselves and puts us into Christ. It's a faith that is so fully persuaded, it acts in a manner consistent with that persuasion.ᵀ⁴² It's a faith that replaces natural human rebellion with a genuine love for the Master. How important is that? Read Mark 12:29-31.¹¹² What are the greatest commandments?

▪

▪

Now, read John 14:15.¹¹³ What is the natural outflow from our love for God?

Obedience is not so much something we *do* but rather how we respond to God's love—a love that will overflow to others. In 1 John 4:7-8,10 we see that we love because He loves.

Beloved, let us love one another, for love is from God; and everyone who loves is born of God and knows God. The one who does not love does not know God, for God is love. . . . In this is love, not that we loved God, but that He loved us and sent His Son to be the propitiation for our sins.

In Christ, then, obedience to God's Word is not an unnatural act of our will but a natural response to the One in whom we *really* believe—the One whom we are able to love because He first loved us (1 John 4:19). Spend a few moments today in prayer. Read Proverbs 13:13, then thank God for His Word and for His gift of love that enables us to joyfully obey His commandments.

BRINGING IT HOME . . .

1. In both the Old Testament and the New Testament, we are called to engage all our faculties toward embracing the gospel. We must:

   - Attune our ears to listen

   - Engage our minds to reason, comprehend, and make application to our own lives

   - Exercise our will to walk in obedience to God's Word

   Which one of these activities is the weakest link in your life as a Christian? Why do you think this is true?

2. Think about your overall, normal response to God's Word. Are you more likely to obey out of a desire to escape the consequences of disobedience or to experience the rewards of obedience? Ask God to reveal to you any places where you are hearing the Word, but not doing the Word. What action(s) do you need to take to change in these areas?

POINT OF INTEREST:[T42]

A PICTURE OF FAITH—
The French tightrope walker Charles Blondin gave us a most dramatic illustration of the gospel's concept of belief. In 1860, Blondin successfully crossed Niagara Falls on a 1,000-foot span of wire, 160 feet above the raging waters. After his first successful crossing, Blondin asked his awestruck audience if they believed he could cross over again, this time pushing a wheelbarrow. The enthusiastic crowd cheered, acknowledging their faith in him. Before a third trip, Blondin asked, "Does anyone believe enough in me to get in the wheelbarrow this time and cross Niagara Falls with me?" No one volunteered! Finally, his manager climbed into the wheelbarrow and they crossed the great chasm together.

The Word tells us that there is a great chasm between us and God. The only way to get across is by believing in Christ so completely that your faith is manifested in reckless obedience to His commands. If you don't trust Him enough to "get in," you don't trust Him enough. (Story adapted from Ken Boa and Larry Moody, *I'm Glad You Asked,* [Victor: Wheaton, IL, 1994], pp. 240-241.)

DAILY READING

Read Proverbs 8:1-9 and mark the proverb that stands out most to you today. Review all the proverbs you marked this week

To the leader: For this session you will use a board or flipchart in activity 4.

1. By now your group should know each other fairly well. Take this opportunity to affirm each other in the areas where you see a reflection of God's character. Have each person write his or her name on the back of a three- by five-inch index card. Rotate the cards around the group and have each person write one Christlike quality on each card about the person named. Distribute the cards at the end of the session.
   - Share wise words from your growing-up years—from parents, other relatives, teachers, or others—that have had a positive impact on you throughout your life.
   - What Scriptures—words from your heavenly Father—have been particularly meaningful to you?

2. Our society says, "Seeing is believing." And yet God says, "So faith [or believing] comes from hearing" (Romans 10:17) and "Now faith is the assurance of things hoped for, the conviction of things not seen" (Hebrews 11:1).
   - Why is it easier to believe in things we can see?
   - What are some of the conditions that must exist before a person can come to Christ in faith for salvation?

3. Read aloud the parable of the sower in Matthew 13:18-23.[96]
   - In what ways might Satan "snatch away" God's Word? How can you help a person who has just heard the gospel and is beginning to doubt or back away from it?
   - How can one be assured he or she has a firm root of faith?
   - What are some of the "worries of the world" that can choke out the Word in your life? How can you safeguard against them?
   - What actions can you (or anyone desiring to know God) take to ensure you hear and understand the Word?
   - What other parallels are there between gardening and sharing your faith with others?

4. Do you agree (A) or disagree (D) with the following statements? Discuss the reasons for your answers.
   - Consistent exposure to an idea or truth will eventually lock that idea in your mind.
   - Worry and faith can coexist.
   - Scripture memory is good, but I can grow spiritually without it.

On the board or flipchart list some of the benefits of meditating on God's Word. Get into pairs and review your memory verses from this study. (You should have at least four verses you are working on.)

5. Our obedience is a measure of our belief. But obedience doesn't come naturally. It is something we learn as a result of submitting to God through the power of the Holy Spirit. The writer of Hebrews tells us, "Although He [Jesus] was a Son, He learned obedience from the things which He suffered. And having been made perfect, He became to all those who obey Him the source of eternal salvation" (5:8-9).
   - What is the difference between hearing the Word and doing the Word?
   - Do you think it is easiest to learn from instruction (knowing God's Word), from observing the lives of others and learning from their mistakes, or from trial and error in your own life?
   - How does obedience relate to the pursuit of wisdom?

Close your group time by distributing the cards you completed at the beginning of today's time together. Then pray that the Lord will help each person to apply the truths from this unit throughout the coming week and beyond.

INTRODUCTION TO UNIT 5

EXHORTING "MY SON"

Destination: To discover how to recognize and overcome common temptations with God's provision of wisdom and power.

In a communications class I (Gail) once attended, the instructor said, "You need to tell them what you are going to tell them. Then tell them. Then tell them what you told them." This process of giving an overview, a detailed discussion, and a summary is the same process the Proverbs father uses to communicate wisdom to the son. In these first nine chapters of Proverbs, the father tells the son what he's "going to tell him." Within these preparatory or overview chapters there are ten separate (oratory) messages by the father, exhorting his son to pursue wisdom. These exhortations, all beginning with "My son," are like little pieces of instruction covering broad categories of life issues. Here is a brief synopsis of Ten Exhortations from the Proverbs father:

I. 1:8-33: Both parents are involved in the teaching. The son is exhorted to avoid wrong companions (specifically, men of violence) and to be aware of the consequences of refusing wisdom.

II. 2:1-22: Father pleads for the son to seek and search for wisdom as for hidden treasure and reminds him of the benefits of wisdom, including deliverance from the evil man and the adulterous woman.

III. 3:1-35: Father exhorts his son to remember his parents' teaching and to hold fast to kindness, truth, and a good reputation. Father also encourages the son to trust in the Lord, not to be wise in his own eyes, and to accept discipline.

IV. 4:1-9: Son is reminded of his wise heritage and is encouraged to prize wisdom and to seek it for himself.

V. 4:10-19: Father explains the importance of an active life-pursuit of wisdom. He also contrasts the sweetness and peace of wisdom with the chaos and anxieties of folly.

VI. 4:20-27: Father tells his son to keep on the straight path. He also deals with issues involving the will and the heart.

VII. 5:1-23: Son is told about the pitfalls of immorality; that is, something desirable in the beginning ends in shame, pain, and death.

VIII. 6:1-19: Father warns of two follies that lead to financial ruin; namely, becoming surety (financial obligation on a speculative deal) and laziness (for example, the sluggard). He also lists seven things that are abominable to the Lord.

IX. 6:20-35: Father shows the consequences of immorality, specifically of extramarital relationships.

X. 7:1–8:36: Folly and Wisdom are personified as two women with contrasting natures. Wisdom in 8:22-31 personifies Christ.

In unit 5 we will focus on the father's warning of some character traits and basic types of people that the son should avoid—people who will serve their own interests to the detriment of others. The father warns that becoming involved in wrong relationships will move the son in a direction of radical rebellion against God. In these preparatory chapters of Proverbs, the father also warns the son of predictable temptations that will make him susceptible to wrong relationships, such as the longing for acceptance, the love of wealth, and the lust of sensuality. This week's study will help you recognize the temptations that are common to sinful people and to understand God's provision for handling those temptations His way.

DAY 1

THE SNARE OF BAD COMPANY

During the early part of our study, we saw that the author, purpose, recipients, and key verse of Proverbs were all presented in the first chapter. The father's first admonition to his son is also in this prominent place. Read Proverbs 1:10-15 followed by 3:31 and 4:14. Who or what is the son being warned to avoid?

Read 1 Corinthians 15:33.[114] The truth of this verse applies to all ages, but especially to the young. Young people who get into trouble, particularly males, usually begin around age twelve or thirteen. What do you think might motivate a young person to align himself (or herself) with wrong companions? What need(s) is this person seeking to have met? (Hint: Revisit Proverbs 1:14.)

At first we might conclude that money is the primary motivator. But young people on the threshold of adulthood have a tremendous need to be accepted, to belong. Boys in this transition period are extremely vulnerable to offers of male camaraderie, particularly from older companions who display pseudo strength and power and who pretend to treat them as equals. Evil men prey on youthful vulnerability, and treachery (drugs, theft, sexual perversion) is almost always involved. As the Proverbs father warns his son in advance, so also must parents warn their own children today.

Read Proverbs 1:15-19. How does the father discredit these potential predators?[T43]

The father calls violent men "stupid; dumber than birds; self-defeating." While they are setting traps for others, they are ambushing their own lives. Aggressors may enjoy temporary gain, the father says, but in the end, their wickedness will cost them everything.

Violent men and criminals are the extremes, but they're not the only characters that the father says to avoid. Read the following Proverbs and write down other types of people who make inappropriate companions.

20:19

22:24-25

24:21

The son is admonished to evaluate the character of people. The criminal element (that is, the ones who lack respect for life and property, who are self-seeking, and who have wrong values) is certainly to be avoided. But so are people who are quick-tempered, slanderers, gossips, and "given to change."

Companions who are prone to anger, gossip, or slander are obvious trouble. But what of people "given to change?" The Hebrew word for "change" here is *shana,* meaning "to alter, disguise, or pervert." People given to change are inconsistent and deceptive. They wear false faces; they have a hidden agenda.

Read Proverbs 13:20 and 14:8. Who else is to be avoided?

Why?

The common denominator among Proverbs' list of unacceptable companions is deception. We'll look at this more closely in the next daily excursion. For now, let's look at a potential dilemma that faces Christians; namely, how can Christians avoid sinners and yet win them to Christ? Write down your personal ideas before going on.

The biblical answer is to look at wisdom incarnate (in the flesh). Jesus was known as a friend of sinners, and He had a powerful impact on them. Jesus called to sinners from open places. He didn't compromise His reputation by going into a brothel to minister, for example; but He laid aside His social status to meet with

POINT OF INTEREST:[T43]

BE *IN* BUT NOT *OF* THE WORLD—Let's be honest. When you hang around with people, after a while they begin to imprint on you; they impact your thinking. A companion of fools soon suffers injury—that's reality. It is wise, therefore, for us to "hang" with people who have some wisdom.

This doesn't mean that we associate only with Christians (be *in* the world but not *of* the world). But it does mean that if we are sufficiently different, the world will be either drawn to us or repelled by us. No one ever remained neutral after encountering Jesus—they either accepted Him or persecuted Him. Christians should expect the same either/or reaction. The question to ask ourselves is this: "Am I different enough, is Christ obvious enough in my life, so that people are either attracted to or repelled by me?" We are not greater than our Master who was mocked, reviled, persecuted, and crucified. When were you last honored by being persecuted f or righteousness sake?

For further study:
Can people be destroyed by association with evil? (Genesis 18:20-32, 19:12-17, 29-30, Numbers 16:23-35) Will Christians be persecuted? (Matthew 5:10-12, John 15:20, 1 Corinthians 4:12, 2 Timothy 3:12)

115 2 CORINTHIANS 6

14-15 Do not be bound *[heterozugeo]* together with unbelievers; for what partnership have righteousness and lawlessness, or what fellowship has light with darkness? Or what . . . has a believer in common with an unbeliever?

116 TITUS 3

10-11 Reject a factious man after a first and second warning, knowing that such a man is perverted and is sinning, being self-condemned.

117 2 JOHN 1

9-11 Anyone who goes too far and does not abide in the teaching of Christ, does not have God. . . . If anyone comes to you and does not bring this teaching, do not receive him into your house, and do not give him a greeting; for the one who gives him a greeting participates in his evil deeds.

118 2 THESSALONIANS 3

14 And if anyone does not obey our instruction in this letter . . . do not associate with him, so that he may be put to shame.

119 1 CORINTHIANS 5

9-11,13 I wrote you in my letter not to associate with immoral people; I did not at all mean . . . people of this world . . . for then you would have to go out of the world. But [do not] . . . associate with any so-called brother if he should be an immoral person, or covetous, or an idolater, or a reviler, or a drunkard, or a swindler—[do] not . . . even eat with such a one. . . . REMOVE THE WICKED MAN FROM AMONG YOURSELVES.

harlots in the open square. There He treated them with compassion. Jesus had the wisdom and knowledge of God, yet He used discretion and remained dependent on the Father. That kept Him clean and moving in the right direction, even when mixing it up with sinners.

While Jesus was a friend of sinners, they were not in His most intimate circles. God sets boundaries for Christians in terms of the extent of their relationships with unbelievers. Read 2 Corinthians 6:14-15.[115]

What relationships are limited by this Scripture?

Why has God set such limits?

The Greek word for "bound," *heterozugeo,* means "to be yoked up differently." Christians must not be *bound* with unbelievers in any partnership (marriage, business, and so on) because they have no common value system. Christ's example teaches us to distance ourselves from the sin without alienating the sinner. There are exceptions. Read Titus 3:10-11,[116] 2 John 1:9-11,[117] 2 Thessalonians 3:14,[118] and 1 Corinthians 5:9-11,13.[119]

Whom should Christians reject, not associate with, or not receive?

Do these people appear to be inside or outside the assembly of believers?

People who cause division (the factious), people who proclaim a false gospel, people who rebel against biblical doctrine, and people who live ungodly lives—yet *claim* to be Christians—are among those with whom Christians must disassociate. All are from *within* the church— "so-called" brothers who profess Christianity but live contrary to the commandments of Christ. We are to recognize and avoid the tares among the wheat,[T44] bearing in mind that the "immoral people of this world" (sinners) are "not at all" included (1 Corinthians 5:9-11).

BRINGING IT HOME . . .

1. All young people are vulnerable to adult predators. What could you do to help prepare your child or a child in your church or community to be more discerning?

2. If you noted a negative change in the attitude or behavior of a child you were close to and you believed that change could be attributed to the company they were keeping, what would you do? Do you believe you have any responsibilities to intervene in the lives of children in the congregation of your church? Why, or why not? Ask God to show you when to intervene in the lives of young people and how to do so with love and caring.

3. As a young person, in what ways were you negatively influenced by the company you kept? What about today? What changes in your associations do you need to make? Ask God to make you discerning and obedient in your own relationships.

HISTORY & CULTURE:[T44]

TARES AND WHEAT—Tares are a kind of grass that is difficult to tell from wheat until it heads. Not only do tares provide no grain (or fruit), they also are host to a fungus that infects its seeds and is poisonous to humans. Note, then, that tares are a significant problem when cohabiting with wheat.

For further study:
What analogy do you see within the church?
(Matthew 13:24-30)

DAILY READING

Read Proverbs 8:10-21. Mark the verse that stands out most to you today.

DAY 2

THE BAIT OF DECEIVERS

[120] JEREMIAH 14

14 Then the LORD said to me, "The prophets are prophesying falsehood in My name . . . a false vision, divination, futility and the deception of their own minds."

[121] PSALM 62

4,9 They delight in falsehood; They bless with their mouth, But inwardly they curse. . . . Men of low degree are only vanity, and men of rank are a lie.

[122] GENESIS 3

13 And the woman [Eve] said, "The serpent deceived me, and I ate."

[123] REVELATION 12

9 And the great dragon was thrown down, the serpent of old who is called the devil and Satan who deceives the whole world.

[124] EPHESIANS 4

7,11-15 But to each one of us grace was given according to the measure of Christ's gift. He gave some as apostles . . . prophets . . . evangelists . . . and . . . pastors and teachers, for the equipping of the saints for the work of service, to the building up of the body of Christ; until we all attain to . . . the knowledge of the Son of God. . . . As a result, we are no longer to be children, tossed here and there by waves, and carried about by every wind of doctrine, by the trickery of men, by craftiness in deceitful scheming; but speaking the truth in love, we are to grow up in all aspects into Him who is the head, even Christ.

In day 1 we discussed Proverbs' list of wrong companions and noted that each one was characterized as a deceiver. Deception is an illusion created intentionally to lead others down a wrong path in order to gain some advantage over them. Deception is often remarkably effective, even on intelligent people, because it is usually laced with some element of truth and it normally plays on another's personal weaknesses or blind spots.

Read Jeremiah 14:14[120] and Psalm 62:4,9.[121] Who are the liars? Deceivers? Imposters?

How does Proverbs 14:25 describe these people?

Deceivers are treacherous, and they are found in all stations in life—from the lowest of the low to people of high degree, from blatantly evil people to religious imposters.

Read the first mention of deception in Genesis 3:13.[122] Who is the deceiver?

Read Revelation 12:9.[123] Who is this serpent?

Read John 8:44.[42] What is he the father of?

Susceptibility to deception (apart from God) showed up early in human history and has remained a fundamental plague, even to this generation. As we learned in unit 2, day 3, we are born with a fallen nature and nurtured on lies so that we simply cannot tell truth from error. In fact, "The heart is more deceitful than all else And is desperately sick; Who can understand it?"

(Jeremiah 17:9). Deceiving or being deceived is inherent in our humanity, yet it has no place in the life of a Christian. What protects us from the trickery of men and equips us for service, according to Ephesians 4:7,11-15?[124]

In addition to the Word of God and the Spirit of truth, our Father has placed us in the body of Christ. Through His Spirit, He has gifted men and women to serve as messengers and mentors one to another. By maturing us in the knowledge of Himself and appointing us to be mutually accountable, God protects us from being tossed about by wrong doctrine and the trickery of men. Therefore Christians need not worry about being deceived if they'll seek God's truth.[T45]

THE MODEL DECEIVER

Proverbs warns against making companions of many types of deceivers but also describes for us a quintessential deceiver—*a worthless person*. Read Proverbs 6:12-14. Everything about this person is false. His whole body language speaks duplicity. Constantly trying to deceive, he says one thing and means another. He can't be open and he never communicates clearly. He lacks integrity and righteousness. He is never really inclined to consider his neighbor's good, but his actions are not overt. He has hidden agendas, usually for the ultimate purpose of gaining a profit. He means to deceive.

Compare this description of the deceiving ways of the "worthless person" with the things God hates (and finds abominable). Read Proverbs 6:12-14, then read Proverbs 6:16-19. Write the key word(s) from each verse listed below that relates to the clue word.

Clue	Worthless Person's Character	What God Hates
mouth	6:12	6:17
feet	6:13	6:18
heart	6:14	6:18
spreads	6:14	6:19

POINT OF INTEREST:[T45]
PEOPLE OF INTEGRITY—
We admire people in whom (in the words of Jesus) there is no guile (deception). Guileless people say what they mean and they mean what they say. You can depend on their "yes" to be yes and their "no" to be no. They are trustworthy, have integrity, and are the same, inside and out. Know anybody like that?

While *we* admire them, the world does not. Low ethics or morals become glaringly exposed against the backdrop of a guileless person. Therefore, honest, open speech and actions are "politically incorrect" and unpopular; and people without guile are often in need of encouragement. If you have friends who are trustworthy, consistent, and full of integrity, why not write them a note telling them how much you appreciate their noble character?

For further study:
John 1:46-47
1 Peter 2:1, 3:10

GOD'S REACTION TO DECEIVERS

The character of the worthless person, which is centered on deception, is an abomination to a God who hates—*detests*—deceptive ways.

Now read Proverbs 6:15. How does God promise to deal with the deceiver?

Many deceivers in the Bible were broken without remedy. Cain killed his brother then lied to God. He was cast from God's presence—made a wanderer. Delilah tricked Sampson into telling her the source of his strength. Her people were destroyed. Judas betrayed Jesus, then hung himself in great remorse.

Scripture reveals deceivers, even among those who had received God's blessings. One of the best-known deceivers in Scripture is Jacob, son of Isaac, grandson of Abraham. In Hebrew, Jacob's name (from *aqeb*) means "to take by the heel; to supplant (to supersede by tripping up another)." Jacob tricked his own father into giving him "the blessing" meant for his older brother Esau. ("The blessing" was God's covenant promise to be passed down through the descendants of Abraham.[T46]) God honored Jacob's ownership of the blessing, but not the means by which he acquired it. Those seeds of deception produced a bitter harvest in his life. Jacob was himself deceived many times, even by those who were closest to him—his uncle Laban, his wife Rachel, even his own sons.

Read Genesis 47:8-9.[125] How does an aged Jacob reflect on his life?

Deception is a serious offense to God—one that will not go unpunished. Read Revelation 21:8.[126] According to this passage, what end will *all* liars face?

Now read Proverbs 8:6-9. In contrast to the deceptive speech of the worthless person, how is Wisdom's speech described?

[125] GENESIS 47
8-9 And Pharaoh said to Jacob, "How many years have you lived?" So Jacob said ". . . few and unpleasant have been the years of my life."

[126] REVELATION 21
8 "But for the . . . unbelieving . . . murderers and immoral persons and sorcerers and idolaters and all liars, their part will be in the lake that burns with fire and brimstone, which is the second death."

Deception is the antithesis of wisdom; therefore, deceiving cannot be a lifestyle of a true child of God. Those whose lives are characterized by deception and lying will be suddenly broken without remedy and will face eternal damnation. If we are wise, then, we will aim to become people in whom there is no guile.

BRINGING IT HOME . . .

The love and forgiveness of the Father are just as available to the one who has been a liar and a deceiver as to the one who has been guilty of drunkenness, adultery, theft—even murder. Reconciliation is made available to us through the sacrifice of the Son. When we are saved, the Holy Spirit begins a process of regeneration whereby those sins of deception become sins of the past.

1. If deceptive behavior was part of your lifestyle before you became a Christian, you may find yourself slipping into old patterns of behavior. Ask God to identify and remove any forms of deceptive behavior in your life. What practical steps can you take to eliminate these behaviors?

2. If you are a Christian and are still haunted by past deceptions, ask God to reveal any circumstances where you need to "right" a wrong. Ask Him also to give you the strength to carry out what He tells you to do.

3. Find a trustworthy Christian friend and ask him or her to hold you accountable for walking in honesty and integrity in every area of your life—work, family, community, church. Schedule a time to meet regularly with this person to discuss progress and to pray. If you already have a relationship of this type, drop a note of thanks to this friend for his or her valuable role in your life.

HISTORY & CULTURE:[T46]

THE ABRAHAMIC BLESSING (Genesis 17)—When Abram was ninety-nine years old, God appeared to him and established with him and his descendants an everlasting covenant (binding promise) to make him a father of a multitude of nations, to bless the world through his offspring and to hold the land of Canaan (now Israel) for an everlasting possession. God stipulated that this blessing should be handed down to Abraham's son Isaac.

In Genesis 25 we read that Issac's wife Rebekah bore twins—Esau first, then Jacob. Isaac was intent on giving "the blessing" to Esau, his firstborn. But Rebekah devised a scheme that Jacob used to trick his blind, aging father into giving him the blessing instead. According to Genesis 25:23, God apparently intended for Jacob to receive the blessing all along, for He told Rebekah that the older twin in her womb would serve the younger. By taking matters into his own hands, however, Jacob bought for himself a life of bitter reaping.

DAILY READING

Read Proverbs 8:22-31. Mark the verse that stands out most to you today.

DAY 3

THE LURE OF RICHES

¹²⁷ 1 TIMOTHY 6

9-10 But those who want to get rich fall into temptation and a snare and many foolish and harmful desires which plunge men into ruin and destruction. For the love of money is a root of all sorts of evil, and some by longing for it have wandered away from the faith, and pierced themselves with many a pang.

A material value system permeates our culture. The pursuit of wealth is a central driving force with most people, even among those who embrace Christian ideologies. Our society may be the worst in its focus on riches, but it certainly is not unique among nations, neither in this present age nor in times past. Greed is a powerful tool of the enemy. Read 1 Timothy 6:9-10.[127]

What is one root of all sorts of evil?

What happens to "those who want to get rich"?

The greatest danger related to the love of money is that it pulls us away from faith. This temptation beckons to each of us, sometimes overtly, sometimes subtly, always lethally. As we saw on day 1 of this unit, the love of money can set us on a destructive path of criminal activity. For most, however, the paths to personal, moral, and financial ruin are more subtle, such as

- becoming surety

- having a poor work ethic

- having an improper attitude about wealth

BECOMING SURETY

"Surety" in Hebrew is *arab* meaning "to take on pledge or give in pledge." Becoming surety means putting oneself into financial obligation without the resources to do so. It involves being attracted to a "deal," and then committing beyond one's possible ability to repay. People who want others to become surety for them are often wheeler-dealers who run on and over the ethical edge. Read Proverbs 6:1-5 and the verses from Proverbs listed below. Write what you learn about those who become surety.

11:15

17:18

22:26-27

In the Hebrew culture, debt obligation was particularly binding because the debtor and his family became the slaves of the person to whom money was owed. Naturally the father would tell the son to do whatever it took to get out of that obligation; to "importune himself, humble himself" (in the Hebrew, "let him walk on you"). In our culture the consequences are not so severe, but the principle remains. This warning may mean (as some suggest) that one should not co-sign on a loan or a bank note. Certainly such caution is implied. But *explicitly*, the proverbs warn that we must not pledge money we aren't prepared to either repay or lose.

OUR WORK ETHIC

The Proverbs father does not condemn wealth but does condemn ill-gotten gain. Likewise, the father does not condemn the poor, but does condemn poverty-inducing behavior. Read the following verses from Proverbs and note what you see regarding diligence and laziness.

Diligence	Laziness
6:10-11	
10:4-5	
12:24	
18:9	
21:5	

Just as the father presents the wise man as a worthy model, so also he contrasts the slacker as a model to be disdained.[T47] To teach the son about the dangers of laziness, the father depicts an almost laughable character— the sluggard. Read Proverbs 20:4, 24:30-34, and 26:13-16 and describe the sluggard in your own words.

The sluggard is one of the tragic comic figures in Proverbs. This person is lazy and laden with excuses for his or her laziness. The sluggard embodies the idea of a soft choice. He or she won't begin things, won't finish things, won't face things, and then believes his or her own excuses. The sluggard is a restless, helpless, and useless character.[T47]

POINT OF INTEREST:[T47]

THE SPIRITUAL SLUGGARD— The sluggard says, "A little sleep, a little slumber, a little folding of the hands to rest . . ." But boy, look at the consequences! We're a bit like the sluggard spiritually. We compromise "a little" here and "a little" there until we deceive ourselves by the smallness of our surrenders. Most people never plan to surrender a lot when they first move toward sin a little. We hear about some pastor or church leader who blew it—all of a sudden. That just can't be. Sin always has a history. It starts with something little that leads to a little more and a little more.

Giving in to sin in small concessions will move a person farther and farther down the wrong path. They think they'll just move from point A to point B, but would never go so far as point Z. Then one day they realize that *point Z* is exactly where they are! Their collapse wasn't a sudden blowout but a slow leak. We are astounding in our ability to rationalize disobedience. But God always knows the truth; and deep down inside, so do we. (Adapted from Derek Kidner, *The Proverbs* [Downers Grove, IL: InterVarsity, 1964], p. 42.)

128 1 THESSALONIANS 4

11-12 Make it your ambition to lead a quiet life and attend to your own business and work with your hands, just as we commanded you; so that you may behave properly toward outsiders and not be in any need.

129 2 THESSALONIANS 3

7-12 For you yourselves know how you ought to follow our example, because we did not act in an undisciplined manner among you, nor did we eat anyone's bread without paying for it, but with labor and hardship we kept working night and day so that we might not be a burden to any of you; not because we do not have the right to this, but in order to offer ourselves as a model for you, that you might follow our example. For even when we were with you, we used to give you this order: if anyone will not work, neither let him eat. For we hear that some among you are leading an undisci-plined life, doing no work at all, but acting like busybodies. Now such persons we com-mand and exhort in the Lord Jesus Christ to work in quiet fashion and eat their own bread.

130 1 TIMOTHY 5

8 But if anyone does not provide for his own, and especially for those of his household, he has denied the faith, and is worse than an unbeliever.

Laziness and negligence are condemned in the New Testament as well as the Old Testament. Read 1 Thessalonians 4:11-12,[128] 2 Thessalonians 3:7-12,[129] and 1 Timothy 5:8.[130]

What fate does Paul recommend for those who will not work?

Who is considered to be worse than an unbeliever?

OUR ATTITUDE ABOUT MONEY

Refusing to work is a great sin. According to Scripture, the lazy should not get to eat and non-providers are worse than unbelievers. Labor is the biblical method for producing prosperity.[T48]

In these preparatory chapters, however, the father is focused less on material prosperity and more on the *enduring* wealth of wisdom. Read Proverbs 3:13-18 and 8:11-20. What "wealth" does wisdom offer? (You may want to review day 4 of unit 4.)

Those who love wisdom are endowed with—filled up with—long life, peace, happiness, understanding, power, sound judgment, justice, and righteousness! Should wis-dom bring material prosperity, the wise will invest it in the kingdom of God. Whether the temptation is for ill-gotten gain, for hoarding, or for consuming material wealth for our own pleasure, we must not be lured by the *love* of riches. It will only lead to ruin.

BRINGING IT HOME . . .

Balance is an important concept throughout Scripture. We are told to work, but not to overwork; and we are told to work as unto the Lord rather than unto man.

1. On a scale of 1 to 10 (with "1" being a total sluggard and "10" being a workaholic), where would you place yourself as a worker? If you are out of balance in either direction, what do you plan to do to reinstate balance in your life? What adjustments do you need to make in your thinking? What actions can you take?

2. The love of money is not *the* source of all evil (pride probably is), but it certainly is *a* source of all kinds of evils that we don't think much about. Is money-making a driver in your life? Do disagreements about the use of money cause friction in your home? Does the material wealth of others cause you to favor them or to envy them? Do you treat the poor with the same respect that you treat those who have material wealth? What other ways do you see money as a potential evil in your life?

3. If you answered yes to one or more of the questions in question 2 above, do a word study on "money," "riches," or "wealth" (see[T4]). Take what you learn about the subject and about yourself to the Lord and ask Him to teach you the right perspective about money and to enable you to trust Him as your ultimate source of provision.

POINT OF INTEREST:[T48]

THE WORKAHOLIC—
We tend to be creatures of extremes. Either work is totally unimportant and we tend to avoid it or else it becomes all important and we tend to be defined and consumed by it. We become human *doings* instead of human beings. As Dr. Richard Swenson writes, people who become consumed with doing, lose all "margin" in their lives. Without margin (adequate discretionary time, energy, and money) we get stressed out, can't think clearly, and don't make good decisions. Urgent matters take precedence over important things in life; and we miss out on relationships and things that make life really have quality. When we idolize our work, we have a different kind of problem. Workaholism is *not* a biblical principle. (If workaholism is an issue in your life, you may want to read *Margin,* by Dr. Richard A. Swenson, an excellent resource published by NavPress.)

DAILY READING

Read Proverbs 8:32-36. Mark the verse that stands out most to you today.

DAY 4

THE TRAP OF SENSUALITY

[131] **MATTHEW 5**

27-28 "You have heard that it was said, 'YOU SHALL NOT COMMIT ADULTERY'; but I say to you, that everyone who looks on a woman to lust for her has committed adultery with her already in his heart."

[132] **JAMES 1**

13-15 Let no one say when he is tempted, "I am being tempted by God"; for God cannot be tempted by evil, and He Himself does not tempt anyone. But each one is tempted when he is carried away and enticed by his own lust. Then when lust has conceived, it gives birth to sin; and when sin is accomplished, it brings forth death.

[133] **EXODUS 34**

6-7 "The LORD God, compassionate and gracious, slow to anger, and abounding in lovingkindness and truth; . . . who forgives iniquity, transgression and sin; yet He will by no means leave the guilty unpunished."

[134] **GALATIANS 6**

7 Do not be deceived, God is not mocked; for whatever a man sows, this he will also reap.

In the ancient Jewish culture, educating a child about sex, including its temptations and implications, was the duty of the parents. In Proverbs we see both parents involved in teaching the son about the trap of sensuality before the world seduces him into its ways. Read Proverbs 2:16 and 5:3-4. Note that the adulteress shares the same common trait of all other wrong companions— deception!

The folly of adultery and the consequences of extramarital relationships are dealt with primarily in the seventh and ninth "my son" exhortations of the father's ten mini-sermons listed on page 95.

Read Proverbs 9:13-18. What do the adulterous women personify?

Proverbs uses female imagery to personify both wisdom and folly. Folly is revealed as an adulteress and as "simple." There are two basic categories of adulterous women that the son is told to avoid: wayward wives and professional harlots. The father distinguishes among wayward wives. Read the verses from Proverbs listed below and write some of the differing characteristics of these women.

2:16-17

5:3-8,20

6:24-29

Did you catch the distinctions? The first wayward wife is in open rebellion. She has left her husband, deliberately ignoring her covenant before God. The second wayward wife, the adulterous woman, appears to be amoral. The word in the Hebrew, *zur,* indicates that she is a stranger and a foreigner. She may be ignorant of God's law, perhaps being from a society (like ours) where sexual promiscuity is a way of life. The third wayward wife is clearly one whose husband is trusting in her fidelity. She is more subtle, cunning, flirtatious, beguiling— and dangerous.

Read the description of the professional harlot in Proverbs 7:5-7,21. How is her "prey" described?

Revisit the gallery of fools on page 42 and you'll find this young man—he's among the *pathim*, the ones who lack judgment. Picture him! He flatters himself about being a man of the world but he doesn't know a thing. He places himself on a harlot's street at twilight, with the dark of night setting in (notice the imagery). He's fooling around with death, deliberately going to the wrong place at the wrong time. You can almost hear him thinking, *I can handle her. . . . I'll just play along a while, then leave.* But this woman has a history. She is shrewd, he is naive. He has already compromised himself. He's in her territory, and she reels him in. It's a lost cause. Does her deception and his naiveté release him from responsibility? Hardly!

Read Matthew 5:27-28[131] and James 1:13-15.[132] Where had the young man's sin already taken place?

This young man has knowingly flirted with temptation and courted his own *self-deception*. How absurd to believe you can play with fire and not get burned. Self-deception leads to the *spiritual delusion* that God will look the other way. We must not kid ourselves! God is by no means unaware. There will be an accounting.

Read Exodus 34:6-7[133] and Galatians 6:7.[134] What will God by no means do or be according to these verses?

Do

Be

Ultimately, we must order our ways before God. He will not leave the guilty unpunished. He will not be mocked. God isn't trying to keep us from enjoying life. In fact, He wants us to have life in abundance, but it never comes by way of self-indulgence. Short-term sensual pleasure brings long-term pain.[T49]

POINT OF INTEREST:[T49]

THE PRICE OF A MORAL HOLIDAY—Out-of-town conferences or conventions can be so dangerous. People sometimes think they're on a moral holiday! Even otherwise moral people will get involved in a *short* deal, believing they will never get caught. Many people in this environment have gotten themselves into extremely compromising situations—even people who attend church and profess to know God.

There is a true account of a man at an out-of-town convention who took someone up on an offer to send up a call girl. That night, when the man answered the anticipated knock on his hotel room door, there stood his own daughter, a university student in a nearby town. In his shock, shame, and horror, all he could say was, "Don't tell your mother; don't tell your mother!" He then slammed the door.

What happened in that moment? All respect for himself and for his daughter was destroyed. All his daughter's respect for her father was destroyed. The family atmosphere from thenceforth became one of shame, silence, and constant terror that the truth would somehow become known. Never, *ever* believe you are on a moral holiday and that no one will know. God will always know, and He is in the business of revealing truth!

For further study:
Luke 8:17, 12:2-3

135 1 CORINTHIANS 10

13 No temptation has overtaken you but such as is common to man; and God is faithful, who will not allow you to be tempted beyond what you are able, but with the temptation will provide the way of escape also, that you may be able to endure it.

136 2 PETER 2

9 "The Lord knows how to rescue the godly from temptation, and to keep the unrighteous under punishment for the day of judgment."

Read about the consequences of illicit sex and adultery in Proverbs 5:4-5, 5:8-14, and 6:32-35. List some of these consequences:

The whole appeal of sexual intimacy outside of the covenant, care, and commitment of marriage is a sensual illusion. As the imagery shows, life is a journey; and sensuality can easily lure the unguarded off the right path. Thousands of years of history and myriad painful experiences confirm that those who yield to immorality, those who use people sexually, are *never* fulfilled. In fact, in their bodies and in their lives they "groan at the latter end, when [their] flesh and [their] bodies are consumed" (Proverbs 5:11). Yet men and women, young and old, still leave God's path of true joy and pleasure for a path of disappointment, emptiness, guilt, disease, ruin, and death. Why do you think this happens?

How can we protect ourselves? Some ways are to fear the Lord (unit 2); acquire and apply wisdom (unit 3); embrace the Word (unit 4); recognize and avoid temptations common to man (unit 5). Write other admonitions from Proverbs in the space below.

2:6-8

3:5-6

4:23

5:18-20

God protects the way and makes the paths straight for those who walk in integrity. Read 1 Corinthians 10:13[135] and 2 Peter 2:9.[136] What does God promise us in relation to temptations?

If we will trust God, He will give us victory.

BRINGING IT HOME . . .

1. Is there any unconfessed sexual sin in your life—from the past or present? If so, confess it to God and ask Him to forgive and cleanse you. Then ask Him to put you on a new course beginning today. From now on, when the Enemy accuses (and he will), thank God for His forgiveness and grace.

   If you feel you have a continuing struggle with sexual temptation, flee its source, pray continually, fast, and find a faithful Christian brother (if you're a man) or sister (if you're a woman) to hold you accountable.

2. Most people think of sexual sin as sexual intimacy outside of the marriage covenant. But sexual sin begins in the mind long before it is acted on in the body. In what ways do you protect your mind from harboring sexual sin and lust? Ask God to show you any other means of defense you can put into place.

3. Are there avenues for sexual sin to enter your home or work? What type of music are you listening to? What about the words to the music you listen to or in the books you read? What do you watch on television, videos, or movies? What sites are you visiting on the Internet? Would you want to share these things with your closest friend? Your spouse? Jesus? If not, what changes do you need to make?

DAILY READING
Read Proverbs 9:1-9. Mark the verse that stands out most to you today.

DAY 5

THE WALK OF THE WISE

[137] GENESIS 39

1,6-10 Now Joseph had been taken down to Egypt; and Potiphar, an Egyptian officer of Pharaoh . . . bought him from the Ishmaelites. . . . So he left everything he owned in Joseph's charge. . . . Now Joseph was handsome in form and appearance. . . . And . . . his master's wife looked with desire at Joseph, and she said, "Lie with me." But he refused and said . . . "How then could I do this great evil, and sin against God?" . . . as she spoke to Joseph day after day, . . . he did not listen to her to lie beside her, or be with her.

[138] GENESIS 39

11-21 [Joseph] went into the house to do his work, and none of the men of the household was there inside. And she [Potiphar's wife] caught him by his garment, saying, "Lie with me!" And he left his garment in her hand and fled, and went outside. . . . So she left his garment beside her until his master came home. Then she spoke . . . "The Hebrew slave, whom you brought to us, came in to me to make sport of me. . . . When his master heard the words of his wife, . . . his anger burned. So Joseph's master took him and put him into the jail, the place where the king's prisoners were confined. . . . But the Lord was with Joseph and extended kindness to him, and gave him favor in the sight of the chief jailer.

Proverbs tells us that those who turn aside from wisdom, hate discipline, spurn correction, and refuse instruction will suffer social ruin, financial ruin, physical harm, and ultimately, death. On the other hand, those who embrace wisdom, insight, discretion, and discipline will be kept secure during temptations because of the promise of God's protection, as revealed in 1 Corinthians 10:13.[135] On days 1-4 we looked at people and passions to be avoided. Let's spend day 5 looking at people and passions to be embraced if we are to become wise men and women.

Tucked among the verses in Proverbs are some insights into character building that we haven't highlighted thus far. Read these verses from Proverbs and summarize the instructions in your own words.

2:20-21

3:3-4

3:5-6

3:7-8

3:11-12

16:7

We have a responsibility to set our course on a wise walk. A wise walk entails more than just avoiding bad company. It includes guarding our own hearts and actively seeking out others whose lives provide an example for us to follow. A wise walk begins when we fear the Lord and acknowledge our own lack of wisdom. A person walking in wisdom trusts that God is seeing to his or her best interests, even when life is contrary to that person's expectations. And a person walking in wisdom will keep his or her eyes on God and accept His discipline as acts of love.

THE WISE WALK OF JOSEPH

To see how godly character plays out in life, let's do a brief study of Joseph.[T50] In Genesis 41:46,[139] Joseph at age thirty is described as being more discerning and wise than anyone else in all of Egypt. Read his story in Genesis 39:1,6-10.[137]

Joseph, a young man full of discretion and wisdom, demonstrated his disciplined life in right response to an adulterous woman. He not only wouldn't lie with Potiphar's wife, he wouldn't even go near her.

Read Genesis 39:11-21.[138] What was the result of Joseph's moral choice?

Though he fled adultery, Joseph still suffered unjustly at the hand of a deceiver. Yet he never became bitter. Instead, he held fast to the sovereignty of God. We might be dismayed if Joseph's story ended in prison. But what Potiphar's wife meant for evil, God meant for good. Read Genesis 41:39-40,46.[139]

Joseph's imprisonment became the career ladder for what God had intended all along. Would Joseph have become a leader and spiritual hero had he not honored God with a wise walk, including honoring God with his body?

WISDOM AND FOLLY

The Proverbs father sums up his appeal to his son by presenting Wisdom as a woman of excellence and Folly as a woman of ill repute. Folly embodies all the characteristics of the adulterous women, as mentioned in the preceding chapters. Compare Proverbs 8:32–9:6 with Proverbs 9:13-18 and Job 20:12-15.[140]

Wisdom	Folly
Proverbs 8:32–9:6	*Proverbs 9:13-18, Job 20:12-15*
Calls from	
Food	
Who turns in	

STUDY TECHNIQUES:[T50]

CHARACTER STUDIES—
Character studies help us understand reasons behind the commandments of God and learn more about the person of Christ. By studying the consequences of obedience and disobedience in a Bible character's life we can better understand the *why* of God's commands. Character studies can also reveal similarities between a character and Christ—that is, traits, heritage, and life experiences.

Joseph is an excellent subject for a character study. His life reveals God's sovereignty, as God turns evil intentions into victory by accomplishing His purposes. Joseph is also a type or foreshadow of Christ. For example, like Christ, Joseph was intended for leadership but was rejected and hated by his jealous brothers. He was a savior of both the Gentiles in Egypt and his own Jewish family. And Joseph fully and freely forgave his brothers when they had wronged him.

To do a simple character study, use a good concordance and look up every reference to the character's name. Make a list or chart of the character's activities, traits, occupation, lineage, and so on. In your reading, always be asking questions like:

- Why is this person noted in the Bible?
- What should we learn from him or her?
- Is God pleased or displeased with his or her life? Why?
- Does this character further God's kingdom or is he or she a hindrance?
- What do I learn about Jesus from this character?

Try a quick character study of Joseph. Start with these Scriptures showing Joseph's lineage: Genesis 11:10–12:9; 17:1-5,9,19; 21:3; 25:20-26; 29:10-12.

¹³⁹ GENESIS 41

39-40,46 So Pharaoh said to Joseph, " . . . there is no one so discerning and wise as you are. You shall be over my house, and according to your command all my people shall do homage; only in the throne I will be greater than you." . . . Now, Joseph was thirty years old when he stood before Pharoah, king of Egypt.

¹⁴⁰ JOB 20

12-15 Though evil is sweet in his mouth, And he hides it under his tongue, Though he desires it and will not let it go, But holds it in his mouth, Yet his food in his stomach is changed To . . . venom.

Wisdom and Folly represent two philosophies, two value systems, two ideas—one divine, one demonic—that are in constant rivalry. Both have prepared a banquet. Wisdom's banquet is hearty, and her table leads to great joy, freedom, and life. But Wisdom's feast is costly. It requires complete dependence and utter surrender to the King. Folly's banquet appeals to our pride and our desire for autonomy, but her feast leads to great sorrow, bondage, and death. Her food will not satisfy for long because it has no substance.

Although the world's system is folly, it will still constantly pull on us because we are wired to control our environment. We become captivated by things we can count, measure, and manipulate. They seem more real to us than that which transcends the earth and is supernatural. But in essence, God says, "Ours is a relationship and you are going to have to trust Me." That trust is based on what God has already done in Christ.

EPILOGUE: CHAPTER 9

In chapter 9, the Proverbs father sums up his exhortations. By comparing Proverbs 1:2-7 and 9:9-12, note how the father begins and ends his teaching. Briefly summarize the main teachings common to both passages:

This dual invitation by Folly and Wisdom and the response of both the wise and foolish tie together the basic themes of Proverbs. The walk of a wise person is characterized by his or her pursuit of wisdom, receiving of instruction, and acceptance of discipline. The walk of the scoffer is characterized both by rejection of wisdom's call and disdain for wise counsel.

Wisdom's banquet illustrates and foreshadows Christ's invitation to us. Jesus offers us life and a relationship with Himself, inviting us to come like children, openhanded, to receive the bread of heaven. He invites us to His banquet—not by works but by grace—to forever receive and drink deeply from Him. How we choose will determine the abundance of our life on earth and the place of our eternal destiny. Our prayer is that *you* will choose wisely.

BRINGING IT HOME . . .

1. In what ways has the knowledge you've gained from God's Word during this study increased your desire to walk in wisdom? What will you do to continue pursuing wisdom?

2. As you recall, discipline is fundamental to attaining wisdom and living in the light of it. How will you apply the wisdom you now have? How will you live it out?

3. Explain what you've learned about wisdom as it relates to salvation. Does your salvation experience parallel what you've seen in Scriptures shared in this study?

   - Have you heard the gospel?
   - Have you received it?
   - As a result, do you desire to obey God's Word?
   - Have you seen evidence in your life that you've repented (both mourned *and* turned from sin)?

If you answered "no" to any of these questions, examine yourself to see if you're really a child of God's kingdom. Turn to appendix B and review God's plan of salvation.

This unit concludes the guided tour study on *Pursuing Wisdom*. While this short study has not plumbed the depths of Proverbs 1–9, it has prepared you, as a serious student, to receive wisdom by increasing your understanding of the Source of wisdom, the work of wisdom, and the Person of wisdom (Jesus Christ). If you've been diligent in *Pursuing Wisdom*, then you'll want to immediately begin the second GUIDEBOOK, *The Art of Living Well: A Biblical Approach from Proverbs*.

DAILY READING
Read Proverbs 9:10-18. Mark the verse that stands out most to you today. Review all the proverbs you marked this week and select one to memorize.

115

To the leader: For this group time, you will use the board or flipchart for question 5.

1. Proverbs (as well as the rest of Scripture) offers much wisdom about the kind of company we should keep. As a group, look up and read the following Scriptures. Then discuss the wisdom about friends found in each text.

   Proverbs 12:26

   Proverbs 22:24-25

   1 Corinthians 15:33

   - It has been said, "The worst enemy is the wrong kind of friend." Do you agree or disagree with this statement? Use any additional Scriptures to support your answer.
   - Reconcile these verses with the idea of being a friend of sinners to win them to the kingdom of God.
   - Contrast this information with John 15:13-14. How do we show that we are friends of Jesus?

2. Deception entered human history when Satan came to Eve in the garden. Ever since, it has been present in one form or another. Think of common forms of deception in our current society. Name as many as you can think of.
   - Which forms of deception seem to be the most effective? What makes people so susceptible to deception (discuss both internal and external forces)?
   - Why do you think deceiving and lying are so high on God's list of things He hates?
   - What will be the consequences of a lifestyle of deceiving?

3. Day 3 of this final unit dealt with the lure of riches. It named three paths to personal, moral, and financial ruin: becoming surety, having a poor work ethic, and having an improper attitude about wealth.
   - *Webster's Dictionary* defines surety as "one who has become legally liable for the debt, default, or failure in duty." What are some modern-day examples of surety?
   - Football Coach Bo Schembechler related that there are two kinds of men he didn't want on his team: Those who would *not* do what he told them and those who would do only what he told them. How does this idea relate to a good work ethic? What are some examples of a good work ethic?
   - One subtle form of self-deception is thinking, *If I just had more money, I'd be happy.* So many people work longer hours or get a second job to pursue material things. What is wrong with this thinking?
   - According to 1 Timothy 6:10, "The love of money is a root of all sorts of evil." How is this verse commonly misquoted? Specifically, what types of evil will the love of money draw someone into?
   - What is the biblical method of acquiring wealth? Why do you think our work is important to God?

4. In our society sensuality is a powerful force to be reckoned with. We are bombarded with double entendres and sensual images by lyrics to songs, advertising, and even news reports.
   - How can we escape from the temptations all around us? Brainstorm for ideas. For each thing to avoid, come up with a positive action to take.
   - There is a tremendous amount of feedback, even in secular society, about the painful consequences of illicit sex—everything from broken families to terminal diseases. Why do you think this information is not deterring men and women from adulterous relationships?

5. Now that you have completed the tour of *Pursuing Wisdom,* think of some ways to continue on the journey. Brainstorm and list ideas on the flipchart or board. Once the list is complete, select one and commit to implementing it.

Close in prayer. Allow time for everyone to ask God for His enabling power to live out what they have learned. Thank God for all you have learned together.

Appendix A—

Readings from Proverbs

Proverbs 1

[1]The proverbs of Solomon the son of David, king of Israel:

[2]To know wisdom and instruction, to discern the sayings of understanding,

[3]To receive instruction in wise behavior, righteousness, justice and equity;

[4]To give prudence to the naive, to the youth knowledge and discretion.

[5]A wise man will hear and increase in learning, and a man of understanding will acquire wise counsel,

[6]To understand a proverb and a figure, the words of the wise and their riddles.

[7]The fear of the Lord is the beginning of knowledge; fools despise wisdom and instruction.

[8]Hear, my son, your father's instruction, and do not forsake your mother's teaching.

[9]Indeed, they are a graceful wreath to your head, and ornaments about your neck.

[10]My son, if sinners entice you, do not consent.

[11]If they say, "Come with us, let us lie in wait for blood, let us ambush the innocent without cause;

[12]Let us swallow them alive like Sheol, even whole, as those who go down to the pit;

[13]We shall find all kinds of precious wealth; we shall fill our houses with spoil;

[14]Throw in your lot with us; we shall all have one purse,"

[15]My son, do not walk in the way with them. Keep your feet from their path,

[16]For their feet run to evil, and they hasten to shed blood.

[17]Indeed, it is useless to spread the net in the eyes of any bird;

[18]But they lie in wait for their own blood; they ambush their own lives.

[19]So are the ways of everyone who gains by violence; it takes away the life of its possessors.

[20]Wisdom shouts in the street; she lifts her voice in the square.

[21]At the head of the noisy streets she cries out; at the entrance of the gates in the city, she utters her sayings:

[22]"How long, O naive ones, will you love simplicity? And scoffers delight themselves in scoffing, and fools hate knowledge?

[23]"Turn to my reproof, behold, I will pour out my spirit on you; I will make my words known to you.

[24]"Because I called, and you refused; I stretched out my hand, and no one paid attention;

[25]And you neglected all my counsel and did not want my reproof;

[26]I will even laugh at your calamity; I will mock when your dread comes,

[27]when your dread comes like a storm, and your calamity comes on like a whirlwind, when distress and anguish come on you.

[28]Then they will call on me, but I will not answer; they will seek me diligently, but they shall not find me,

[29]Because they hated knowledge, and did not choose the fear of the Lord.

[30]"They would not accept my counsel, they spurned all my reproof.

[31]"So they shall eat of the fruit of their own way, and be satiated with their own devices.

[32]"For the waywardness of the naive shall kill them, and the complacency of fools shall destroy them.

[33]"But he who listens to me shall live securely, and shall be at ease from the dread of evil."

Proverbs 2

[1]My son, if you will receive my sayings, and treasure my commandments within you,

[2]Make your ear attentive to wisdom, incline your heart to understanding;

³For if you cry for discernment, lift your voice for understanding;

⁴If you seek her as silver, and search for her as for hidden treasures;

⁵Then you will discern the fear of the LORD, and discover the knowledge of God.

⁶For the LORD gives wisdom; from His mouth come knowledge and understanding.

⁷He stores up sound wisdom for the upright; he is a shield to those who walk in integrity,

⁸Guarding the paths of justice, and He preserves the way of His godly ones.

⁹Then you will discern righteousness and justice and equity and every good course.

¹⁰For wisdom will enter your heart, and knowledge will be pleasant to your soul.

¹¹Discretion will guard you, understanding will watch over you,

¹²To deliver you from the way of evil, from the man who speaks perverse things;

¹³From those who leave the paths of uprightness, to walk in the ways of darkness;

¹⁴Who delight in doing evil, and rejoice in the perversity of evil;

¹⁵Whose paths are crooked, and who are devious in their ways;

¹⁶To deliver you from the strange woman, from the adulteress who flatters with her words;

¹⁷That leaves the companion of her youth, and forgets the covenant of her God;

¹⁸For her house sinks down to death, and her tracks lead to the dead;

¹⁹None who go to her return again, nor do they reach the paths of life.

²⁰So you will walk in the way of good men, and keep to the paths of the righteous.

²¹For the upright will live in the land, and the blameless will remain in it;

²²But the wicked will be cut off from the land, and the treacherous will be uprooted from it.

PROVERBS 3

¹My son, do not forget my teaching, but let your heart keep my commandments;

²For length of days and years of life, and peace they will add to you.

³Do not let kindness and truth leave you. Bind them around your neck, write them on the tablet of your heart,

⁴So you will find favor and good repute in the sight of God and man.

⁵Trust in the LORD with all your heart, and do not lean on your own understanding.

⁶In all your ways acknowledge Him, and He will make your paths straight.

⁷Do not be wise in your own eyes; fear the LORD and turn away from evil.

⁸It will be healing to your body, and refreshment to your bones.

⁹Honor the LORD from your wealth, and from the first of all your produce;

¹⁰So your barns will be filled with plenty, and your vats will overflow with new wine.

¹¹My son, do not reject the discipline of the LORD, or loathe His reproof,

¹²For whom the LORD loves He reproves, even as a father, the son in whom he delights.

¹³How blessed is the man who finds wisdom, and the man who gains understanding.

¹⁴For its profit is better than the profit of silver, and its gain than fine gold.

¹⁵She is more precious than jewels; and nothing you desire compares with her.

¹⁶Long life is in her right hand; in her left hand are riches and honor.

¹⁷Her ways are pleasant ways, and all her paths are peace.

¹⁸She is a tree of life to those who take hold of her, and happy are all who hold her fast.

¹⁹The LORD by wisdom founded the earth; by understanding He established the heavens.

²⁰By His knowledge the deeps were broken up, and the skies drip with dew.

²¹My son, let them not depart from your sight; keep sound wisdom and discretion,

²²So they will be life to your soul, and adornment to your neck.

²³Then you will walk in your way securely, and your foot will not stumble.

²⁴When you lie down, you will not be afraid; when you lie down, your sleep will be sweet.

²⁵Do not be afraid of sudden fear, nor of the onslaught of the wicked when it comes;

²⁶For the LORD will be your confidence, and will keep your foot from being caught.

²⁷Do not withhold good from those to whom it is due, when it is in your power to do it.

²⁸Do not say to your neighbor, "Go, and come back, and tomorrow I will give it," when you have it with you.

²⁹Do not devise harm against your neighbor, while he lives in security beside you.

³⁰Do not contend with a man without cause, if he has done you no harm.

³¹Do not envy a man of violence, and do not choose any of his ways.

32For the crooked man is an abomination to the LORD; but He is intimate with the upright.

33The curse of the LORD is on the house of the wicked, but He blesses the dwelling of the righteous.

34Though He scoffs at the scoffers, yet He gives grace to the afflicted.

35The wise will inherit honor, but fools display dishonor.

PROVERBS 4

1Hear, O sons, the instruction of a father, and give attention that you may gain understanding,

2For I give you sound teaching. Do not abandon my instruction.

3When I was a son to my father, tender and the only son in the sight of my mother,

4Then he taught me and said to me, "Let your heart hold fast my words. Keep my commandments and live;

5Acquire wisdom! Acquire understanding! Do not forget, nor turn away from the words of my mouth.

6"Do not forsake her, and she will guard you; love her, and she will watch over you.

7"The beginning of wisdom is: Acquire wisdom; and with all your acquiring, get understanding.

8"Prize her, and she will exalt you. She will honor you if you embrace her.

9"She will place on your head a garland of grace. She will present you with a crown of beauty."

10Hear, my son, and accept my sayings, and the years of your life will be many.

11I have directed you in the way of wisdom; I have led you in upright paths.

12When you walk, your steps will not be impeded; and if you run, you will not stumble.

13Take hold of instruction; do not let go. Guard her, for she is your life.

14Do not enter the path of the wicked, and do not proceed in the way of evil men.

15Avoid it, do not pass by it; turn away from it and pass on.

16For they cannot sleep unless they do evil; and they are robbed of sleep unless they make someone stumble.

17For they eat the bread of wickedness, and drink the wine of violence.

18But the path of the righteous is like the light of dawn, that shines brighter and brighter until the full day.

19The way of the wicked is like darkness; they do not know over what they stumble.

20My son, give attention to my words; incline your ear to my sayings.

21Do not let them depart from your sight; keep them in the midst of your heart.

22For they are life to those who find them, and health to all their whole body.

23Watch over your heart with all diligence, for from it flow the springs of life.

24Put away from you a deceitful mouth, and put devious lips far from you.

25Let your eyes look directly ahead, and let your gaze be fixed straight in front of you.

26Watch the path of your feet, and all your ways will be established.

27Do not turn to the right nor to the left; turn your foot from evil.

PROVERBS 5

1My son, give attention to my wisdom, incline your ear to my understanding;

2That you may observe discretion, and your lips may reserve knowledge.

3For the lips of an adulteress drip honey, and smoother than oil is her speech;

4But in the end she is bitter as wormwood, sharp as a two-edged sword.

5Her feet go down to death, her steps lay hold of Sheol.

6She does not ponder the path of life; her ways are unstable, she does not know it.

7Now then, my sons, listen to me, and do not depart from the words of my mouth.

8Keep your way far from her, and do not go near the door of her house,

9Lest you give your vigor to others, and your years to the cruel one;

10Lest strangers be filled with your strength, and your hard-earned goods go to the house of an alien;

11And you groan at your latter end, when your flesh and your body are consumed;

12And you say, "How I have hated instruction! And my heart spurned reproof!

13"And I have not listened to the voice of my teachers, nor inclined my ear to my instructors!

14"I was almost in utter ruin In the midst of the assembly and congregation."

15Drink water from your own cistern, and fresh water from your own well.

16Should your springs be dispersed abroad, streams of water in the streets?

¹⁷Let them be yours alone, and not for strangers with you.

¹⁸Let your fountain be blessed, and rejoice in the wife of your youth.

¹⁹As a loving hind and a graceful doe, let her breasts satisfy you at all times; be exhilarated always with her love.

²⁰For why should you, my son, be exhilarated with an adulteress, and embrace the bosom of a foreigner?

²¹For the ways of a man are before the eyes of the LORD, and He watches all his paths.

²²His own iniquities will capture the wicked, and he will be held with the cords of his sin.

²³He will die for lack of instruction, and in the greatness of his folly he will go astray.

PROVERBS 6

¹My son, if you have become surety for your neighbor, have given a pledge for a stranger,

²If you have been snared with the words of your mouth, have been caught with the words of your mouth,

³Do this then, my son, and deliver yourself. Since you have come into the hand of your neighbor, go, humble yourself and importune your neighbor.

⁴Do not give sleep to your eyes, nor slumber to your eyelids.

⁵Deliver yourself like a gazelle from the hunter's hand, and like a bird from the hand of the fowler.

⁶Go to the ant, O sluggard. Observe her ways and be wise,

⁷Which, having no chief, officer or ruler,

⁸Prepares her food in the summer, and gathers her provision in the harvest.

⁹How long will you lie down, O sluggard? When will you arise from your sleep?

¹⁰"A little sleep, a little slumber, a little folding of the hands to rest"—

¹¹And your poverty will come in like a vagabond, and your need like an armed man.

¹²A worthless person, a wicked man, is the one who walks with a false mouth,

¹³Who winks with his eyes, who signals with his feet, who points with his fingers;

¹⁴Who with perversity in his heart devises evil continually, who spreads strife.

¹⁵Therefore his calamity will come suddenly; instantly he will be broken and there will be no healing.

¹⁶There are six things which the LORD hates; yes, seven which are an abomination to Him:

¹⁷Haughty eyes, a lying tongue, and hands that shed innocent blood,

¹⁸A heart that devises wicked plans, feet that run rapidly to evil,

¹⁹A false witness who utters lies, and one who spreads strife among brothers.

²⁰My son, observe the commandment of your father, and do not forsake the teaching of your mother;

²¹Bind them continually on your heart; tie them around your neck.

²²When you walk about, they will guide you. When you sleep, they will watch over you; and when you awake, they will talk to you.

²³For the commandment is a lamp, and the teaching is light; and reproofs for discipline are the way of life,

²⁴To keep you from the evil woman, from the smooth tongue of the adulteress.

²⁵Do not desire her beauty in your heart, nor let her catch you with her eyelids.

²⁶For on account of a harlot one is reduced to a loaf of bread, and an adulteress hunts for the precious life.

²⁷Can a man take fire in his bosom, and his clothes not be burned?

²⁸Or can a man walk on hot coals, and his feet not be scorched?

²⁹So is the one who goes in to his neighbor's wife; whoever touches her will not go unpunished.

³⁰Men do not despise a thief if he steals to satisfy himself when he is hungry;

³¹But when he is found, he must repay sevenfold; he must give all the substance of his house.

³²The one who commits adultery with a woman is lacking sense; he who would destroy himself does it.

³³Wounds and disgrace he will find, and his reproach will not be blotted out.

³⁴For jealousy enrages a man, and he will not spare in the day of vengeance.

³⁵He will not accept any ransom, nor will he be content though you give many gifts.

PROVERBS 7

¹My son, keep my words, and treasure my commandments within you.

²Keep my commandments and live, and my teaching as the apple of your eye.

³Bind them on your fingers; write them on the tablet of your heart.

⁴Say to wisdom, "You are my sister," and call understanding your intimate friend;

⁵That they may keep you from an adulteress, from the foreigner who flatters with her words.

⁶For at the window of my house I looked out through my lattice,

⁷And I saw among the naive, I discerned among the youths, a young man lacking sense,

⁸Passing through the street near her corner; and he takes the way to her house.

⁹In the twilight, in the evening, in the middle of the night and in the darkness.

¹⁰And behold, a woman comes to meet him, dressed as a harlot and cunning of heart.

¹¹She is boisterous and rebellious; her feet do not remain at home;

¹²She is now in the streets, now in the squares, and lurks by every corner.

¹³So she seizes him and kisses him, and with a brazen face she says to him:

¹⁴"I was due to offer peace offerings; today I have paid my vows.

¹⁵"Therefore I have come out to meet you, to seek your presence earnestly, and I have found you.

¹⁶"I have spread my couch with coverings, with colored linens of Egypt.

¹⁷"I have sprinkled my bed with myrrh, aloes and cinnamon.

¹⁸"Come, let us drink our fill of love until morning; let us delight ourselves with caresses.

¹⁹"For the man is not at home. He has gone on a long journey;

²⁰He has taken a bag of money with him. At full moon he will come home."

²¹With her many persuasions she entices him, with her flattering lips she seduces him.

²²Suddenly he follows her, as an ox goes to the slaughter, or as one in fetters to the discipline of a fool,

²³Until an arrow pierces through his liver, as a bird hastens to the snare, so he does not know that it will cost him his life.

²⁴Now therefore, my sons, listen to me, and pay attention to the words of my mouth.

²⁵Do not let your heart turn aside to her ways, do not stray into her paths.

²⁶For many are the victims she has cast down, and numerous are all her slain.

²⁷Her house is the way to Sheol, descending to the chambers of death.

PROVERBS 8

¹Does not wisdom call, and understanding lift up her voice?

²On top of the heights beside the way, where the paths meet, she takes her stand;

³Beside the gates, at the opening to the city, at the entrance of the doors, she cries out:

⁴"To you, O men, I call, and my voice is to the sons of men.

⁵"O naive ones, discern prudence; and, O fools, discern wisdom.

⁶"Listen, for I shall speak noble things; and the opening of my lips will produce right things.

⁷"For my mouth will utter truth; and wickedness is an abomination to my lips.

⁸"All the utterances of my mouth are in righteousness. There is nothing crooked or perverted in them.

⁹"They are all straightforward to him who understands, and right to those who find knowledge.

¹⁰"Take my instruction, and not silver, and knowledge rather than choicest gold.

¹¹"For wisdom is better than jewels; and all desirable things can not compare with her.

¹²"I, wisdom, dwell with prudence, and I find knowledge and discretion.

¹³"The fear of the LORD is to hate evil; pride and arrogance and the evil way, and the perverted mouth, I hate.

¹⁴"Counsel is mine and sound wisdom; I am understanding, power is mine.

¹⁵"By me kings reign, and rulers decree justice.

¹⁶"By me princes rule, and nobles, all who judge rightly.

¹⁷"I love those who love me; and those who diligently seek me will find me.

¹⁸"Riches and honor are with me, enduring wealth and righteousness.

¹⁹"My fruit is better than gold, even pure gold, and my yield than choicest silver.

²⁰"I walk in the way of righteousness, in the midst of the paths of justice,

²¹To endow those who love me with wealth, that I may fill their treasuries.

²²"The LORD possessed me at the beginning of His way, before His works of old.

²³"From everlasting I was established, from the beginning, from the earliest times of the earth.

²⁴"When there were no depths I was brought forth, when there were no springs abounding with water.

^{25}"Before the mountains were settled, before the hills I was brought forth;

^{26}While He had not yet made the earth and the fields, nor the first dust of the world.

^{27}"When He established the heavens, I was there, when He inscribed a circle on the face of the deep,

^{28}When He made firm the skies above, when the springs of the deep became fixed,

^{29}When He set for the sea its boundary so that the water should not transgress His command, when He marked out the foundations of the earth;

^{30}Then I was beside Him, as a master workman; And I was daily His delight, rejoicing always before Him,

^{31}Rejoicing in the world, His earth, and having my delight in the sons of men.

^{32}"Now therefore, O sons, listen to me, for blessed are they who keep my ways.

^{33}"Heed instruction and be wise, and do not neglect it.

^{34}"Blessed is the man who listens to me, watching daily at my gates, waiting at my doorposts.

^{35}"For he who finds me finds life, and obtains favor from the LORD.

^{36}"But he who sins against me injures himself; all those who hate me love death."

PROVERBS 9

^{1}Wisdom has built her house; she has hewn out her seven pillars.

^{2}She has prepared her food, she has mixed her wine; she has also set her table.

^{3}She has sent out her maidens, she calls from the tops of the heights of the city:

^{4}"Whoever is naive, let him turn in here!" To him who lacks understanding she says,

^{5}"Come, eat of my food, and drink of the wine I have mixed.

^{6}"Forsake your folly and live, and proceed in the way of understanding."

^{7}He who corrects a scoffer gets dishonor for himself, and he who reproves a wicked man gets insults for himself.

^{8}Do not reprove a scoffer, lest he hate you, reprove a wise man and he will love you.

^{9}Give instruction to a wise man and he will be still wiser, teach a righteous man and he will increase his learning.

^{10}The fear of the LORD is the beginning of wisdom, and the knowledge of the Holy One is understanding.

^{11}For by me your days will be multiplied, and years of life will be added to you.

^{12}If you are wise, you are wise for yourself, and if you scoff, you alone will bear it.

^{13}The woman of folly is boisterous, she is naive, and knows nothing.

^{14}And she sits at the doorway of her house, on a seat by the high places of the city,

^{15}Calling to those who pass by, who are making their paths straight:

^{16}"Whoever is naive, let him turn in here," and to him who lacks understanding she says,

^{17}"Stolen water is sweet; and bread eaten in secret is pleasant."

^{18}But he does not know that the dead are there, that her guests are in the depths of Sheol.

The following verses from Proverbs are referenced in this study.

CHAPTER 10

^{4}Poor is he who works with a negligent hand, but the hand of the diligent makes rich.

^{5}He who gathers in summer is a son who acts wisely, but he who sleeps in harvest is a son who acts shamefully.

^{8}The wise of heart will receive commands, but a babbling fool will be thrown down.

^{21}The lips of the righteous feed many, but fools die for lack of understanding.

^{27}The fear of the LORD prolongs life, but the years of the wicked will be shortened.

CHAPTER 11

^{2}When pride comes, then comes dishonor, but with the humble is wisdom.

^{15}He who is surety for a stranger will surely suffer for it, but he who hates going surety is safe.

CHAPTER 12

^{23}A prudent man conceals knowledge, but the heart of fools proclaims folly.

^{24}The hand of the diligent will rule, but the slack hand will be put to forced labor.

^{26}The righteous is a guide to his neighbor, but the way of the wicked leads them astray.

CHAPTER 13

^{1}A wise son accepts his father's discipline, but a scoffer does not listen to rebuke.

13The one who despises the word will be in debt to it, but the one who fears the commandment will be rewarded.

19Desire realized is sweet to the soul, but it is an abomination to fools to depart from evil.

20He who walks with wise men will be wise, but the companion of fools will suffer harm.

25The righteous has enough to satisfy his appetite, but the stomach of the wicked is in want.

CHAPTER 14

8The wisdom of the prudent is to understand his way, but the folly of fools is deceit.

9Fools mock at sin, but among the upright there is good will.

16A wise man is cautious and turns away from evil, but a fool is arrogant and careless.

25A truthful witness saves lives, but he who speaks lies is treacherous.

26In the fear of the LORD there is strong confidence, and his children will have refuge.

CHAPTER 15

5A fool rejects his father's discipline, but he who regards reproof is prudent.

20A wise son makes a father glad, but a foolish man despises his mother.

33The fear of the LORD is the instruction for wisdom, and before honor comes humility.

CHAPTER 16

5Everyone who is proud in heart is an abomination to the LORD; Assuredly, he will not be unpunished.

6By lovingkindness and truth iniquity is atoned for, and by the fear of the LORD one keeps away from evil.

7When a man's ways are pleasing to the LORD, he makes even his enemies to be at peace with him.

18Pride goes before destruction, and a haughty spirit before stumbling.

CHAPTER 17

18A man lacking in sense pledges, and becomes surety in the presence of his neighbor.

25A foolish son is a grief to his father, and bitterness to her who bore him.

CHAPTER 18

2A fool does not delight in understanding, but only in revealing his own mind.

6A fool's lips bring strife, and his mouth calls for blows.

9He also who is slack in his work is brother to him who destroys.

CHAPTER 19

28A rascally witness makes a mockery of justice, and the mouth of the wicked spreads iniquity.

29Judgments are prepared for scoffers, and blows for the back of fools.

CHAPTER 20

3Keeping away from strife is an honor for a man, but any fool will quarrel.

4The sluggard does not plow after the autumn, so he begs during the harvest and has nothing.

19He who goes about as a slanderer reveals secrets, therefore do not associate with a gossip.

CHAPTER 21

5The plans of the diligent lead surely to advantage, but everyone who is hasty comes surely to poverty.

24"Proud," "Haughty," "Scoffer," are his names, who acts with insolent pride.

CHAPTER 22

4The reward of humility and the fear of the LORD are riches, honor and life.

6Train up a child in the way he should go, even when he is old he will not depart from it.

10Drive out the scoffer, and contention will go out, even strife and dishonor will cease.

24Do not associate with a man given to anger; or go with a hot-tempered man,

25Lest you learn his ways, and find a snare for yourself.

26Do not be among those who give pledges, among those who become sureties for debts.

27If you have nothing with which to pay, why should he take your bed from under you?

CHAPTER 24

9The devising of folly is sin, And the scoffer is an abomination to men.

21My son, fear the LORD and the king; Do not associate with those who are given to change.

[30]I passed by the field of the sluggard, and by the vineyard of the man lacking sense;

[31]And behold, it was completely overgrown with thistles, its surface was covered with nettles, and its stone wall was broken down.

[32]When I saw, I reflected upon it; I looked, and received instruction.

[33]"A little sleep, a little slumber, a little folding of the hands to rest,"

[34]Then your poverty will come as a robber, and your want like an armed man.

CHAPTER 26

[12]Do you see a man wise in his own eyes? There is more hope for a fool than for him.

[13]The sluggard says, "There is a lion in the road! A lion is in the open square!"

[14]As the door turns on its hinges, so does the sluggard on his bed.

[15]The sluggard buries his hand in the dish; he is weary of bringing it to his mouth again.

[16]The sluggard is wiser in his own eyes than seven men who can give a discreet answer.

CHAPTER 27

[22]Though you pound a fool in a mortar with a pestle along with crushed grain, yet his folly will not depart from him.

CHAPTER 28

[26]He who trusts in his own heart is a fool, but he who walks wisely will be delivered.

CHAPTER 29

[9]When a wise man has a controversy with a foolish man, the foolish man either rages or laughs, and there is no rest.

[20]Do you see a man who is hasty in his words? There is more hope for a fool than for him.

[23]A man's pride will bring him low, but a humble spirit will obtain honor.

APPENDIX B—

GOD'S PLAN OF SALVATION

In America today, most people either do not know what it means to be saved or do not understand that salvation is something they urgently need. God's plan of salvation is good news only when we understand the really bad news: namely, that all of us have broken God's law and the consequences are eternally serious.[141] As a result of Adam and Eve's rebellion, something happened not just *to* them but *in* them that continues to have a residual effect on us—their descendants. It is as if Adam acquired *bad blood* that was passed to all generations. Our inherited sin nature places each of us at odds with a pure and holy God.

Without a *spiritual transfusion*, our condition will end in eternal death (hell).[142] Within the context of this bad news, the tremendous good news of the gospel is fully realized. Through the cleansing power of the blood of Jesus Christ, God has made a way of escape.

Because Jesus was God the Son, His death on the cross satisfied—made propitiation for—the sin debt for all people.[143] This means that the ransom price for your sentence of eternal death has already been deposited into your account by Christ.[144] Whatever amount you need to be reconciled to God is available to you through His Son—and through Him alone.[145] When you come to Jesus, He will require one thing—that you yield your life to be spiritually born anew in Him.[146] So how does one go about being born anew?

1. BEGIN WITH AN HONEST AND SINCERE HEART

God knows exactly where you are and what you think and feel about Him. Therefore, you're free to—indeed you must—tell Him the truth. If you're not sure God exists, tell Him. Then ask Him to reveal Himself to you that you may fully believe in Him. If you don't like

[141] ROMANS 3
23 For all have sinned and fall short of the glory of God.
ROMANS 6
23 For the wages of sin is death, but the free gift of God is eternal life.

[142] ROMANS 5
12 Therefore, just as through one man sin entered into the world, and death through sin, and so death spread to all men, because all sinned.

[143] 1 JOHN 2
2 And He Himself is the propitiation for our sins; and not for ours only, but also for those of the whole world.

[144] ROMANS 3
24-26 [We are] justified as a gift by His grace through the redemption which is in Christ Jesus; whom God displayed publicly as a propitiation in His blood through faith . . . in the forbearance of God He passed over the sins previously committed; . . . that He might be just and the justifier of the one who has faith in Jesus.

[145] ACTS 4
12 There is salvation in no one else; for there is no other name [besides Jesus] under heaven that has been given among men, by which we must be saved.

[146] **1 PETER 1**

23 For you have been born again not of seed which is perishable but imperishable, that is, through the living and abiding word of God.

1 PETER 3

18 For Christ also died for sins once for all, the just for the unjust, having been put to death in the flesh, but made alive in the spirit.

[147] **1 PETER 2**

2 Like newborn babes, long for the pure milk of the word, that by it you may grow in respect to salvation.

[148] **ROMANS 3**

10-12 As it is written, "THERE IS NONE RIGHTEOUS, NOT EVEN ONE; THERE IS NONE WHO UNDERSTANDS, THERE IS NONE WHO SEEKS FOR GOD; ALL HAVE TURNED ASIDE, TOGETHER THEY HAVE BECOME USELESS; THERE IS NONE WHO DOES GOOD, THERE IS NOT EVEN ONE."

[149] **1 JOHN 1**

9 If we confess our sins, He is faithful and righteous to forgive us our sins and to cleanse us from all unrighteousness.

[150] **2 CORINTHIANS 7**

10 For the sorrow that is according to the will of God produces a repentance without regret, leading to salvation; but the sorrow of the world produces death.

[151] **EPHESIANS 2**

8-9 For by grace you have been saved through faith; and that not of yourselves, it is the gift of God; not as a result of works, that no one should boast.

reading His Word or you think His principles are too demanding or you don't like going to church, tell Him. Ask Him to help you through your resistance and to create a desire to know Him through His Word and through His people.[147] Whatever it is that has kept you from coming to God—pride, fear, shame, guilt, anger, disappointment, unbelief, lack of knowledge—tell Him about it and ask Him to bring you to a place of acceptance of His will in your life.

2. CONFESS YOUR SIN AND ASK GOD'S FORGIVENESS

See yourself among the *all* who have sinned.[141] Don't get sidetracked by focusing on your good points or by comparing yourself favorably to others—even to Christians. Don't confuse religious habits, such as church attendance or Christian service, with evidence of your own goodness. When measured against a pure and holy God, all human righteousness is worthless. Agree with God's Word that you are a sinner, and acknowledge your failed efforts at being good. [148] Confess the specific sins you are aware of, such as pride, jealousy, prejudice, intellectualism, anger, rebellion, or anything you see in your life that is unlike Christ.[149] Ask God to make you aware of any hidden sins and convict you of sin until you are truly and deeply sorry for displeasing Him.[150]

3. RECOGNIZE THAT YOU CANNOT SAVE YOURSELF

Understand that you need Someone to do *in* you what you cannot do in and for yourself.[151] You cannot save yourself, call yourself to God, change yourself, or even *really* believe in God by your own efforts.[152] In fact, you can't even desire to come to God by your own intent.[153] But this is great news. It means that any flicker of interest you have toward knowing God is evidence that He is calling you personally to Himself. Your part is to respond to His calling and to yield to His rule and reign in your life. You can trust Him for He is interested only in your highest good.

4. Watch for Evidence of Change from the Inside Out

Don't try to be good. Instead look for changes of the heart—different attitudes, greater love, peace, kindness, joy that spill out in changes in behavior.[154]

Be intentionally introspective—the changes may be subtle at first. Be still before the Lord and allow yourself to sense His presence and His peace. Ask God to let others see changes in you as confirmation that He is at work in your life. If you sense no changes or see no evidence of the Spirit in your life, go back to God and ask Him to reveal anything that may be holding you away from receiving His gift of eternal life. Go through each of these processes again and tell God you will continue seeking Him until He enables you to seek Him with your *whole* heart that He might be found by you, according to His promise.[155] As you grow in your walk with the Lord, both your awareness of sin and your wonder at the Cross will increase.

Meditate on the Scriptures in the side columns. You may want to pray them back to God as *your* own words, from *your* heart. Be assured: He is waiting and He will answer you.

Note: When you pray to receive Christ, seek out a Bible-believing church for fellowship, prayer, Bible study, and accountability.

[152] **John 15**

16 "You did not choose Me [Jesus], but I chose you, and appointed you, that you should go and bear fruit, and that your fruit should remain."

[153] **John 6**

37,44 "All that the Father gives Me shall come to Me, and the one who comes to Me I will certainly not cast out. No one can come to Me, unless the Father who sent Me draws him; and I will raise him up on the last day."

[154] **2 Corinthians 5**

17 Therefore if any man is in Christ, he is a new creature; the old things passed away; behold, new things have come.

[155] **1 Timothy 4**

16 Persevere in these things; for as you do this you will insure salvation both for yourself and for those who hear you.

BIBLIOGRAPHY

Boa, Ken and Larry Moody. *I'm Glad You Asked.* Wheaton, IL: Victor, 1994.

Kidner, Derek. *The Proverbs.* Downers Grove, IL: InterVarsity, 1994.

Martin, William C. *The Layman's Bible Encyclopedia.* Nashville, TN: The Southwestern Company, 1964.

McQuilkin, J. Robertson. *Understanding and Applying the Bible.* Chicago: Moody, 1983.

Precept Ministries. *The International Inductive Study Bible.* Eugene, OR: Harvest House, 1993.

Strong, James. *The New Strong's Exhaustive Concordance of the Bible.* Nashville, TN: Thomas Nelson, 1984.

Teasdale, Sara. "Wisdom" from *Collected Poems.* New York: Macmillan, 1994.

Tenney, Merrill C., general editor. *The Zondervan Pictorial Bible.* Nashville, TN: The Southwestern Company, 1974.

Vine, W. E. , Merrill F. Unger, William White, Jr. *Vine's Expository Dictionary of Biblical Words.* Nashville, TN: Thomas Nelson, 1985.

Zodhiates, Spiros. *The Hebrew-Greek Key Study Bible.* Chattanooga, TN: AMG Publishers, 1990.

Kenneth Boa writes a free monthly teaching letter called Reflections. If you would like to be on the mailing list, call: 800-DRAW-NEAR (800-372-9632).